what others a
about **Good Kids . . .**

"David Hertweck captures the struggle many of us have in youth ministry as we try to define the metrics by which we evaluate the success of our ministries. He provides practical steps to go beyond behavior to a deeper, transformative practice of youth ministry. Whether you're new to youth ministry or a veteran, you'll find something here that will encourage and inspire you to better youth ministry."

—Mark Matlock

president, Youth Specialties; author of many books including Raising Wise Children *and* Living A Life That Matters; *www.youthspecialties.com*

"Leadership isn't the task of simply providing answers. Often, it's about reframing questions. That's exactly what David does in a heartfelt way in *Good Kids*. I trust this book will be one you go back to time and time again as a needed reminder of what questions to ask. I hope you go through it with your team and help them to think, grow, and lead more effectively. I also pray that this will make a difference not only in your ministry but in your heart."

—Doug Fields

bestselling author of multiple books, including Purpose-Driven Youth Ministry; *cofounder of Downloadyouthministry.com*

"*Good Kids* doesn't promise easy answers . . . it delivers on biblical ones. It doesn't promise a sexy splash that magnetizes a teenager's interest . . . it delivers Spirit-directed motivation that will endure the test of time. And perhaps even more life-giving, it doesn't call for the youth leader to be a talented, golden-tongued orator who is a standup comic during "off hours." Instead, it calls for every youth leader to carefully align their priorities and patterns in youth ministry up against the New Testament and take their cues solely from there."

—Jeanne Mayo

president, youth leader's coach, director and founder, "The Cadre"; director of Youth & Young Adult Ministries, Victory World Church, Atlanta, Georgia; speaker, leadership coach, and author

"I'm thankful that my friend, David Hertweck, is talking about the need to evaluate the health of youth ministry. In *Good Kids* he challenges us to go deeper to really know if we're making lifelong disciples of our students. The challenge isn't easy. We might not like what we find. But as David says, students' lives are at stake. We can't afford not to take this challenge and change this conversation."

—Scotty Gibbons

national youth ministries strategist, National Leadership and Resource Center, General Council of Assemblies of God, author of The Big Ten: A Quick-Access Guide to Youth Ministry Essentials

"How does something so primary to the church as the gospel message of Jesus get lost along the way? Dave Hertweck skillfully and compassionately points the church back to the true good news: the person of Jesus Christ. Church leaders need to put this book on their must-read list and then apply the principles in their ministries to generate spiritual transformation in every Christ-follower."

—Garland Owensby, DED Min

Professor, Bible & Church Ministries,
Southwestern Assemblies of God University

"For youth leaders everywhere, David Hertweck has given us a tool that will help us be honest about how we engage with the ministry God has given us. From behavior modification to the music we use in our worship services, David sheds light on some of the reasons teenagers find our meetings less than compelling. If you're ready to take an honest look at what your work is actually producing, get out your pen and paper while you read this. Together, we can set higher standards for our gatherings that will ultimately help students see Jesus."

—Andy Braner

president, KIVU, author of ALONE: Finding Connection in a
Lonely World, *speaker and dreamer*

"Have you ever asked yourself as a youth pastor or youth leader, 'Are we building a student ministry that's actually making disciples?' If that question resonates with you, read this book! In *Good Kids, Big Events, & Matching T-Shirts*, David Hertweck explores how we evaluate success in youth ministry by bringing it back to the main point: making disciples. David provides questions that youth leaders should ask themselves about gospel fluency, Spirit dependency, and biblical community. I love the inclusion of concrete tips from youth leaders nationwide to help develop these three vital characteristics within a youth ministry context. You'll laugh, you'll pause and reflect, and you'll get hungry (Dave is a foodie!), but most importantly, you'll be reminded of what a true gospel-centered youth ministry looks like!"

—Tyler Sollie

network youth director, Northwest Ministry Network

"The conversation surrounding youth ministry changed a long time ago. The travesty is that many still aren't addressing it. David provides a fresh perspective to those who are both engaged and disengaged from the landscape of faith and adolescence. The tension between the gospel and what we think we know will become either a challenge or a catalyst for the days ahead. In *Good Kids* David makes it clear that for leaders willing to ask the hard questions the days ahead are bright. I'm immensely thankful for David's voice in this evolving conversation. I highly recommend this book!"

—Heath Adamson

national youth director, National Leadership and Resource Center, General Council of the Assemblies of God

"David Hertweck has opened the door for an important conversation on the fundamental goals of youth ministry. We need to revisit the metrics and methods of the past in light of the shifting culture of the American church. The new metrics of gospel fluency, Spirit dependency, and biblical community this book offers will help focus the future of youth ministry in a healthy direction. While this new conversation will look different everywhere, the language David introduces in this new book can guide any youth ministry toward a fuller expression of what it looks like for students to live as disciples of Jesus Christ in the twenty-first century. I'm honored to call this gifted author a ministry friend and brother."

—Matt Rule
district youth director, South Texas Youth Ministries

"Throughout the years, we've seen several trends in youth ministries. Some have helped youth ministry; others have hurt it. But one thing is certain. Our congregations and communities are in extreme need of youth groups equipped with the essential Christ-centered tools needed to raise up generations of young leaders and servants willing to follow Jesus Christ and to lift up His name wherever they go. The future pastors, teachers, ministers, politicians, lawyers, doctors, mothers, and fathers will come from today's youth ministries. That's why Bible-centered foundations are vital for the education and growth of these future leaders. In *Good Kids* David Hertweck provides youth ministries with imperative foundations to establish healthy youth groups for the present and the future."

—Eddie Zaldana
district youth director, Spanish Eastern District

"David Hertweck is a gifted leader, communicator, and author. This book is a must-read for every youth leader who wants their young people to embrace a lifelong pursuit of following Jesus.

David brings an urgent, relevant, and much-needed message that will benefit every person who works with young people. Be prepared to be inspired, provoked, and equipped—you won't finish this book disappointed."

—Kent Hulbert
Youth Alive

"This book is a must-read for anyone serious about doing youth ministry in this culture. David is candid, sharing experiences from his personal life and years of youth ministry. You'll find the book both informative and transformational, as it offers practical ways to help students fall in love with Jesus. In short, this book is about grace; we're helpless without the grace of God. David gets that. I recommend this book for every youth pastor and youth worker."

—Omar C. George
Church of God New York, state youth and discipleship director

Good Kids,
Big Events, &
Matching T-Shirts

Changing the Conversation
on Health in Youth Ministry

David Hertweck

MY HEALTHY CHURCH
MyHealthyChurch.com

erin elizabeth.

*One of the most convincing evidences of
God's grace at work in my life is the fact that
I get to share it with you. I love you.*

contents.

foreword.

I've had the wonderful opportunity to serve in youth ministry for more than thirty years, and for the majority of that time I've enjoyed the incredible privilege of contributing my voice to the conversation surrounding youth ministry as a leader and resource provider. I've seen dozens of youth ministry trends come and go. Some have added real value while others have been nothing more than a passing fad. Throughout all that action, the one commonality in each trend is the renewed hope that it will help a youth worker or youth ministry become more healthy and effective.

The desire to understand what a healthy youth ministry looks like isn't a recent development. From the start, youth leaders have been trying to determine what actions will generate measurable results. The pursuit of answers is never-ending: *How do I help teenagers grow in their faith? How can I teach in a way that doesn't bore everyone in the room? How do I explain to a parent that their child was injured playing a game involving frozen turkeys and a Slip' n Slide?*

Along the way, I've learned that when the conversation around health is built on the wrong premises, the conclusion is doomed from the start. If we're aiming at the wrong target, then even if we hit it, we still don't become healthy or successful. Prompting good behavior ("fix my kid"), providing great experiences ("keep them happy and safe"), and promoting group unity ("help them develop friends") have always been seen as some of the important goals in youth ministry.

But what if those primary goals are actually part of the problem?

That's the haunting question my friend David Hertweck is bold enough to address. David has been in youth ministry for fifteen years and currently serves as the youth director in New York for the Assemblies of God. He and I met when he invited me to Syracuse to be part of an event he helped organize. Since then we've connected at several other youth ministry training events, and he's been a regular guest blogger for me at the website I cofounded, Downloadyouthministry.com. In addition to hanging out around youth ministry-type events, we also hang out around food. David is a "foodie" and has introduced me to some amazing food around New York, including the unforgettable soup dumplings in Flushing, Queens. I've learned that his passion for great eating spots is only (and barely!) surpassed by his passion for helping youth leaders create and sustain disciple-making environments. I'm honored to call him a ministry friend and brother.

This book helps bring definition to the necessary elements of any disciple-making environment. David writes in an engaging and easy-to-understand way as he unpacks the values of gospel fluency, Spirit dependency, and biblical community. The chapters focusing on those three values are loaded with thought-provoking insights that may challenge long-held assumptions. Chances are you won't agree with everything in this book, but the journey of re-evaluating certain biases and presuppositions is always a valuable one if you're going to be a credible leader. I think you'll especially appreciate and benefit from the lists of practical suggestions. Leadership isn't the task of simply providing answers. Often, it's about reframing questions. That's exactly what David does in a heartfelt way in this book.

I've been blessed to speak to and share life with many teenagers. To this day, every Wednesday night a group of high school boys comes to my house for a small group. The joy of watching a teenager "get" the gospel and grow in faith is indescribable. But the most important task I've ever had in youth ministry has happened in my home. My wife, Cathy, and I have raised three teenagers (if that's not hardcore youth ministry, then nothing is). Anything you learn in this book about disciple making in youth ministry will serve you in your home, with your own children. And when it's all said and done, that's what matters most.

I trust this book will be one you return to time and time again as a needed reminder of what questions to ask. I hope you go through it with your team and cause them to think, grow, and lead more effectively. I also pray that this will not only make a difference in your ministry, but also a difference in your heart.

—Doug Fields
Author of multiple books, including Purpose-Driven Youth Ministry[1]
Cofounder of Downloadyouthministry.com

chapter one.

KEEPING SCORE

S ome things are just hard to watch:

- The junior higher who talks with her mouth full—your will to live fading with every additional glimpse of partially chewed pizza.

- The awkwardness of the teenage years—using words they can't pronounce, telling jokes they don't understand, or wearing clothes that don't match their personality—or just plain don't match!

- The pain all over the face of that youth group kid as you drive him to the nearest ER because you just ran over his leg with your car. (What? No one else ever did that?)

But as a dad of three little girls, I've encountered something much more difficult to watch than any of those: little kids playing organized soccer. Calling it "organized" is a funny joke at best and a cruel joke at worst. Calling it "soccer" is borderline abuse of the English vocabulary.

Still, every Saturday morning, parents drag themselves and their sleepy-eyed children out to a grassy field to endure an hour or more of watching young kids run as a pack all over the field. Sometimes the soccer ball is actually involved in the action. When you're really lucky, someone actually kicks the ball in the right direction. And every once in a blue moon, the ball actually trickles into a goal and all the parents celebrate wildly, trying to convince themselves this whole endeavor was worth it.

After her first game, I asked my then four-year-old daughter, Lilia, if she had fun. She said "yes," but I think that had more to do with the fact that she was holding her post-game tasty snack and sugary drink in her hands. As I poked and prodded some more, I realized that Lilia had no clue about the final score of the game. She gave me a number, but it was way higher than the real score. Normally, that's not a big deal—what four-year old would know that? But three details about my daughter gave me pause:

1. Lilia is incredibly observant—notices everything!

2. She's very competitive—I'd say she gets that from her mom, but I want the credit for it . . . in case someone is keeping score.

3. I'm half Korean, so she's a quarter Korean—being good with numbers is our thing.

The next part of our conversation revealed the fatal flaw in her score tallying approach. For some reason, she believed that every time the goalie picked up the ball with her hands, the defending team earned a goal. While that creates some interesting strategy, it clearly was the wrong way to keep score. So I took it upon myself to teach her the right way to keep score. If she had the wrong understanding of how to measure success in a soccer game, it would have huge impact on the way she played (I envisioned her repeatedly passing the ball to her own goalie) and how she felt about the game (I imagined her celebrating like a lunatic every single time her goalie picked up the ball).

IS YOUR YOUTH MINISTRY WINNING?

In life, there are few arenas where winning doesn't matter. We keep score at sporting events, we get grades in school, and we even go online to rate the places we visit or the restaurants where we eat. Keeping score in soccer is pretty simple, but keeping score in life can be a real mystery. Youth ministry is no exception—how do we evaluate and assess success in youth ministry? Like soccer (even if it's a game between four-year-olds), the right metrics in youth ministry matters! The way we assess it has a completely unavoidable and remarkably powerful influence on how we do ministry—and how we feel about it. I think we would all agree that success in youth ministry looks like a healthy youth ministry. So when we talk about success, we're really talking about health. Whether you like it or not, *everyone* is evaluating the health of your student ministry. Here's just a starter list:

- You
- Your spouse
- Your volunteers
- Your senior pastor
- Your church board
- Your teenagers
- Visiting teenagers
- The parents of teenagers (yikes!)
- The church custodian (Spoiler alert: He thinks you're a failure every time he has to clean Silly String off another piece of church furniture.)

So many voices and opinions are trying to shape the way you assess your youth ministry. How do you sort through those voices and make sure the bull's eye you're aiming at is actually the right one?

When I was a youth pastor, I had all sorts of ways to evaluate the health of our youth ministry. When it came to our weekly large group gathering, I looked at attendance, number of visitors, energy in the room, how the student band did, how engaged kids were during the talk, and any sort of response. I had seasons where the bar was set high, and a great night meant a huge crowd and some really powerful moments. Then there were times when the bar was lower, and a successful night was not losing my temper on stage at the chatty crowd and not having any brawls between students.

Some of my metrics revolved around facilities and technology: Does the room look cool? Are the basketballs in the gym inflated properly? How many light bulbs were broken tonight? How many toilets were clogged up? Are the couches holding up under the years of severe abuse at the hands and feet of hyper teenagers? Did the media work well? Did the movie clip I showed connect well with the students?

I also evaluated the effectiveness of our adult leaders: Did they show up? On time? Did they connect with students or just talk to each other? If they had on-stage responsibilities, did they do a good job? Were they helping our student ministry teams? Did they bring any snacks to share with me?

So many voices and opinions are trying to shape the way you assess your youth ministry.

Lastly, I evaluated myself. Did I feel engaged with students? Was I fully present in conversations? Did I prepare my volunteers well for their responsibilities? Was I funny at the right times and serious at the right times? Did I preach well? Did I steward the opportunity to speak to these teenagers whom Jesus loves? Did my deodorant hold up?

You get the idea. All of those questions would simultaneously run through my mind in a matter of minutes as I drove home from another youth service. I asked similar questions (and new ones) when it came to evaluating the success of mission trips or outreaches or fun outings or small groups or . . . you name it. Measuring health and success—there's just no avoiding it.

THREE GAME-CHANGING QUESTIONS

In my fifteen-plus years of experience in youth ministry, I've found that youth workers often ask the same three common questions when it comes to measuring the health of their ministry. In this book, I want to consider the potential shortcomings and dangers of these questions and suggest that we add three different questions to help us rethink our metrics for assessing and evaluating the health of our youth ministries.

This would be a good time for me to pause and be transparent: I don't look back on my years in local church youth ministry and view myself as a great success by either set of metrics. I'm no expert. I'm a fellow learner—still with much to learn. I'm not writing as someone standing above you on an invisible stage—pontificating about everything you're doing wrong and why I know better. If it sounds that way sometimes, please know it's a direct result of my passion for seeing healthy, disciple-making youth ministries. I'm writing as someone who's coming alongside you and making discoveries *with* you. It's interesting to note that in the sports world the best coaches often weren't the greatest players—they were okay, but nothing special. I hope that I'm better at helping you think through what you're doing in youth ministry than I was at what I actually did in youth ministry.

The three primary questions that I relied upon in youth ministry were:

CHAPTER ONE: KEEPING SCORE

1. Do the young people behave?

2. Are they having the right experiences?

3. Do they like each other?

In chapters 2, 4, and 6 of this book, we'll take a close look at the potential problems with only using those questions to measure health. Chapters 3, 5, and 7 will introduce three values essential to new metrics: gospel fluency, Spirit dependency, and biblical community. And you'll also find practical ideas from current practitioners to help you move in that direction. I didn't want to suggest these shifts without giving you practical ways to carry them out.

> *Everything I say in this book requires two layers of hard work on your part: consideration and contextualization.*

I should be clear upfront that I'm not advocating for a complete abandonment of existing metrics. Good kids, big events, and matching T-shirts can still be indicators of a healthy youth ministry. What I am suggesting is that they can't be the only indicators—and that as indicators, they benefit from a broader and deeper perspective. Keep in mind that everything I say in this book requires two layers of hard work on your part: consideration and contextualization. Take time to consider if you agree—and if you do, take even longer to understand what this might mean in your specific ministry context. Then find people to journey with you. My hope is that the conversation will engage your mind and your heart and that together we can move forward in responding to the command of Christ to make healthy disciples.

WHAT'S AT STAKE

After Lilia's soccer game, I finally realized why she had been confused about how to keep score. If you've ever had the misfortune of attending a four-year-old's soccer game, then you know that each and every parent standing on the sideline takes turns shouting for their own kid—especially when God miraculously intervenes and their kid actually does something slightly resembling a soccer move. But there are only two times in a game when the entire sideline celebrates.

One occasion is when a goal is actually scored. This is usually the indirect result of the mass group somehow heading in the right direction and the direct result of the goalie counting the petals on a flower while the ball rolls past her. The other time everyone cheers is when the goalie picks up the ball with her hands. That's when it hit me.

Lilia was standing on the field, hearing and watching all the parents cheer every time the goalie successfully picked up the ball. In her brilliant little quarter-Korean brain, she thought to herself, *They're celebrating. So this must count.*

When we talk about measuring the health of our youth ministries, our students are most at stake. We will celebrate the wins—we will cheer for the moments of success. But unless our celebrations are discerning, our students will believe the wrong things count. And that has enormous implications for how they live out their faith.

Measuring our ministry health definitely matters. It's always happening. It eventually shapes students. So it's worth having a conversation about. Thanks for picking up this book and joining the conversation.

Good Kids

chapter two.

OH, BEHAVE!

*F*or any parent, one of the rites of passage is a child's epic meltdown in broad daylight. The feelings of helplessness and hopelessness are only eclipsed by the overwhelming sensations of shame and embarrassment—and that's even before you start getting "the look" from the judgmental passersby. Inevitably, the progression of interaction from the desperate parent to the defiant child goes something like this:

1. Explanation

2. More explanation (louder and slower)

3. Reasoning

4. Reasoning quickly abandoned

5. Threats

6. More threats (quieter and faster)

7. Bribes

8. Begging

If you're a parent, a bit of advice: Just skip straight to No. 8. When I try to place my unwilling two-year-old in the grocery cart seat, she has this amazing ability to morph her body into something resembling the shape and strength of a surfboard. The irony is that when I need her to stand up straight (which her surfboard talents reveal she can clearly do!), she loses all control of her muscles and melts into a puddle of tears and sinful rebellion on the floor. And in these moments, all I really want is for my daughter to behave—like a good little girl, in a way that won't humiliate her dad.

DO THEY BEHAVE?

For many years, this was the primary question I asked when it came to measuring health in youth ministry. "They" were the teenagers in the youth group. The behavior I was looking for could be broken down into two categories: "actions" and "activities." Let me give you a snapshot of what some of these questions look like when we drill down even further.

Actions.

Do students act like well-behaved teenagers? Do they make right choices? Do they listen to certain music, go to certain movies, and say certain words? Do they stay out of trouble, follow the rules, and respect their elders? Do they look like Christian teenagers?

Do they pray and read their Bibles? Do they raise their hands in the right moments during the singing? Do they come forward in response at the end of the sermon?

Activities.

Do they attend youth group regularly? Are they involved in our programs? Do they choose church activities over school activities? Do they choose youth group over a job? Do they go on mission trips, show up for youth outings, or get plugged into our small groups? Are they on our student leadership team or student ministry teams?

When our students appeared to be healthy by the standards of actions and activities, I felt really successful at having a healthy youth ministry. When teenagers behaved well and showed glimpses of spiritual maturity, there was a tangible sense of approval from parents, church leadership, and the church as a whole. I would hear remarks like, "It's amazing how much these teenagers love to worship." Or, "We're so proud of these students for going on a mission trip." Or, "It's been two months since they've 'accidentally' set anything on fire." In other words, we're proud because they behave.

WHY BEHAVIOR?

Along the way, I've discovered some very appealing reasons why we embrace the metric of behavior as a primary indication of our health. Let me share three of them.

1. Behavior is easy to measure.

Behavior is visible, making it measurable. In a world that loves to quantify everything, outward actions and activities provide youth leaders with a tangible metric. If you have a competitive streak in you—and I do—then you love to measure. I don't even understand playing a game if no one keeps score. What's the point? That desire to know the score can easily work its way into youth ministry. It doesn't take much work to get a head count on a Wednesday night, and it doesn't require profound insight to know which kids are making the wrong choices. (They're the ones on your worship team—just kidding! Sort of.) Human beings also love to measure because we love to know where we stand. Our perception of how healthy our ministry is becomes a source of validation. (More on that later.)

> *Our perception of how healthy our ministry is becomes a source of validation.*

2. Measuring behavior addresses the pressures we feel.

Parents often focus on the actions while pastors and church leadership focus on the activities. The average parent is thrilled with the youth ministry if it keeps their son out of jail and their daughter away from an unhealthy dating relationship. If the teenagers in the group look like good Christians, then the youth pastor looks like the second coming of Jesus (I'm using that phrase in the least eschatological sense possible). Senior pastors and church boards might convey expectations of a full youth room and attractive events. It may seem that the surest path to job security is managing the behavior of young people—and sadly, you might be right.

3. It's what we're used to.

People tend to default to what they're familiar with, what they're comfortable with—which in churches often means, "What worked for me should work for you." Many of us grew up in churches where behavior was the only focus. Our faith was defined mostly in terms of what we did. The way to secure the approval of others and God was to live right. If God used that sort of environment to rescue you and call you into youth ministry, then you might assume the same will work for others. You may have endured and even thrived in an environment of legalism. If so, that's the grace of God; your experience doesn't validate that ministry approach. We have to remind ourselves that sometimes God works through us, but He's always working in spite of us. In other words, He might work through ministry styles that aren't healthy simply because He's big enough and good enough to do so. But that doesn't mean we should stay there.

These are just a few of the reasons the question "Do they behave?" has become a primary metric for measuring the health and success of youth ministry. Youth pastors get hired and fired based on their ability to attract a crowd and then convince that crowd to live right. But there are potentially some real problems when this value becomes a primary measurement of our health.

POTENTIAL PROBLEMS

1. To change the behavior of teenagers, you don't need the gospel.

You don't need the good news about Jesus to get students to live differently or to make better choices. From what I can observe, Mormonism produces well-behaved, committed, and religiously active young people. It's typical for Mormon high school graduates to give two years to missions work—that's very commendable behavior. Mormons tend to be respected members of the community, good citizens, and faithful churchgoers. But they don't believe the gospel and its full narrative.

Another example. The military is remarkably effective at changing the behavior of young men and women. These recruits come to boot camp from all over the country, with different backgrounds, personalities, and preferences; and after a few months they all look, sound, and act the same. They behave exactly as they've been trained to behave. But it isn't because they've had a heart-level encounter with Jesus. So clearly there are lesser motivations that even a youth pastor can appeal to in order to change behavior. That's a problem.

2. You'll do or say anything to change behavior.

If the primary way you know that you're a successful youth pastor with a healthy ministry (and a good leader) is when your teenagers live like Christians and attend events, you'll look for any and every way to manufacture that result—even ignoring, bypassing, or perverting the gospel. This strategy or approach manifests itself in relatively innocent ways, like promoting lots of cool giveaways or promising fun and food in an attempt to draw a crowd. It could also sound like a very heartfelt emotional appeal to students, pleading with them to reconsider their poor choices.

> *When behavior becomes the goal, the end justifies the means—"whatever it takes" becomes the mantra.*

It can also be seen in more destructive forms: emotionally manipulating the audience to get them to respond to the sermon, or making students feel like lesser members of the group because their sport or school responsibilities prevent them from attending every youth group event. When behavior becomes the goal, the end justifies the means—"whatever it takes" becomes the mantra. But this means abandoning the "uniquely Christian" approach to change and instead adopting unhealthy methods. (More on that later.)

3. You'll be a slave to the ups and downs of teenage behavior.

I'm not telling you anything new when I say that kids and teenagers are erratic in their behavior. It's not just about spiritual issues—there are physiological reasons, too. I'm not an expert on adolescent development, but it doesn't take much research to realize that the journey of individualization and even the formation of certain decision-making abilities are both still in process for teenagers. The inconsistencies in their lives stem from many factors. Deciding to evaluate and measure their health in terms of their outward behavior is like chaining yourself to a roller coaster created and operated by a lunatic. When our emotional well-being and our sense of calling and effectiveness are tied too closely to the lives of those we serve, we'll never be on solid ground—especially in youth ministry.

MORALISM AND MOTIVATIONALISM

These three problems will splinter off into many other problems, and together they end up creating a culture where behavior is highlighted, celebrated, and rewarded. The approaches leading to this can be painfully obvious or dangerously subtle. For many years in local church youth ministry, I relied on two specific approaches: moralism and what I call "motivationalism" (yes, I realize it's not a word).

Here's the difference between the two. Moralism is birthed out of the desire to *instruct*; motivationalism is birthed out of the desire to *inspire*. You can instruct with moralistic commands: Don't lie, treat others well, don't do bad things. And you can use countless Bible stories to illustrate good and bad examples of those things. This form of moralism tells teenagers: You should . . . ! At that point, we're not gospel proclaimers; we're the morality police.

You also can inspire with tools like stories, emotion, lights, music, and causes. And you can use countless Bible verses to inspire teenagers to believe in themselves, to achieve more, to be better than others. These motivational forms tell teenagers: You can . . . ! At that point, we're not gospel proclaimers; we're cheerleaders.

We must understand that the greatest danger with these two approaches lies in how moralism and motivationalism position the teenager at the center of their own salvation. They end up thinking of being a Christian more in terms of what they do than what Jesus has done. These kinds of approaches appeal to our self-salvation tendencies. Through the years, I've learned that the primary motivations for doing right are self-justification (prove myself) and self-preservation (protect myself). In Luke 18, Jesus tells a parable about rightly motivated religious activity and wrongly motivated religious activity, because He knew there were some in His audience who "were confident of their own righteousness and looked down on everyone else" (Luke 18:9). Moralism and motivationalism fail to highlight the truth that God saved us "not because of righteous things we had done, but because of his mercy" (Titus 3:5). The underlying message here is filled with hints and undertones of earning God's grace and proving our own goodness.

The motivations that align closely with moralism and motivationalism are pride and fear, respectively. Pride says we must prove ourselves, while fear says we must protect ourselves. And as you've probably already discovered, pride and fear are powerful motivations—they can manufacture right behavior. If you're a parent, you probably depend on this!

As a young Christian kid growing up in the 1980s, I had two great fears. One was hell. I would lie in bed at night trying to wrap my mind around eternity and what it would be like to exist in a reality that never, ever ended. Then I would think about what it would be like for that to happen in the fires of hell, tormented by Satan and demons and worms, oh my! It's a miracle I ever slept.

My other great fear was the rapture—more specifically, missing the rapture. I grew up attending watch night services, which always included a potluck dinner, board games, and praying and singing as midnight approached. At some point, we watched one of those terrifying 1970s end-times films. All I remember about them is that they involved people getting decapitated because they refused to take the mark of the beast. I was paralyzed by the thought of being left behind. On occasion, I would come home and couldn't find my parents or siblings. I would immediately panic and begin to quietly and quickly move around the house looking for any signs they were in fact still on planet Earth and not 15,000 feet in the air on their way to glory, shaking their heads at the fact that I'd been left behind.

So as you can imagine, much of my right living and religious activity was motivated by fear. I wanted to protect myself from hell or from having to choose between my head being attached to my body and a tattoo on my right hand or forehead. Very little of my behavior had any connection to a growing, vibrant love for Jesus. In fact, being motivated by fear led to self-preservation-based motivations, which was just another way of saying I loved myself, my comfort, and my well-being—and the current location of my head.

As I got older, I didn't exactly get rid of the fear motivation—I simply added to it. I began to draw more on pride and the desire to prove myself. I wanted to prove to my parents that I was a good son, to my teachers that I was a good student, and to the people in my church that I was a good, well-behaved, spiritually mature young man worthy of their notice and applause. Even the best things I did were motivated by a desire to be seen, to elevate myself, and to separate myself from all the lesser losers. Instead of self-preservation (or in addition to it), I turned to self-justification—works righteousness. I thought my performance secured the approval of others, and I needed that approval because I didn't sense the unconditional approval of God. The reason for that? My erratic performance before God.

As a teenager, I focused on my behavior in all areas. On the rare day I did my devotions, prayed for longer than two minutes, and didn't say or do anything I wouldn't say or do in front of my parents, I felt like a Christian rock star. I felt secure in my standing before God because of my behavior—not because of my understanding of the gospel. On the much more common day when I played video games instead of reading my Bible and didn't remember to pray until I was falling asleep, I wondered exactly where I stood with God. My bedtime prayer was like a last-ditch attempt to clear the slate and hope that God would be okay with that. My relationship with God was all about my ability to behave right and perform well. There wasn't much joy in it. Actually, there was a lot of guilt and shame. And guilt and shame are not tools of the gospel.

I can think back to my teenage years and recall all the different ways I tried to protect myself and prove myself through good behavior. I still remember being in ninth grade, sitting in study hall and dreaming up big plans with my friends. It was 1992, and we all knew the Summer Olympics were coming to Atlanta in four years—we were determined not to miss our opportunity to be there. The typical collaborative brilliance of ninth grade guys kicked in, and we came up with a plan:

- We would form a band.
- We would become famous.
- We would book gigs in Atlanta during summer 1996.
- We would attend the Summer Olympic events during our off time.

I know what you're thinking . . . fail-safe plan, right? Believe it or not, our plan had some holes, not the least of which was the reality that none of us played a musical instrument. But we weren't easily deterred; each of us picked an instrument to learn and off we went. My mom moved to America from South Korea as a teenager. When she arrived, she had trouble making friends, so she bought an acoustic guitar to help her pass the time. I remembered that guitar, lying in the attic, so I went home and began to mess around on it.

Fast-forward a couple years. I had learned four chords and purchased a capo. That meant I was fully equipped to play any worship song (or country song, for that matter). I began leading worship at my home church, and people seemed to like it. I soon realized that the quickest path to gaining the approval and applause of people I respected was to serve the local church with my meager musical skills. Most adults would have looked at my behavior and assumed I was a mighty man of God—at least compared to the teenagers sitting in the back row of the sanctuary. But if you could have looked into my heart, you would have seen that what I really loved and treasured was the approval of others. And I found a way to get it—through good behavior.

In youth ministry, it's crucial that we come face to face with the truth that some teenagers behave not because they love Jesus, but because they love the benefits that come with good behavior. In this case, Jesus isn't

If you could have looked into my heart, you would have seen that what I really loved and treasured was the approval of others.

a beautiful treasure; He's a useful tool. He's not what their hearts desire most; He helps them get what their hearts desire most— approval, attention, control, power, feelings of superiority, or security. It could be anything. Literally, anything can become an idol in our lives. And the treacherous nature of idolatry is that the idols usually aren't inherently bad, nor does idolatry always result in bad behavior. Idols can produce good behavior when the context nurtures it. But in a different context, idols can quickly shift and produce destructive behavior. Sound like any recent high school graduates you know?

FOUR TELLING RESPONSES

How do you know if you're preaching moralism or motivationalism? What signs can you look for that indicate you're calling students to behave more than you're inviting them to believe or behold? When I thought back to my years of being a teenager who relied on works-righteousness, I realized I had four primary responses to moralistic and motivational preaching. My guess is you'll probably recognize yourself and/or your students in one or more of these.

1. Defiant: *I never get this right, and I don't care.*

This teenager listens to you tell him what to do, crosses his arms, and says he doesn't care what you say. It's his life and he's going to live however he wants. You preach a message on dating and challenge teens to start living pure, and he's thinking, *You don't know what it's like to be a teenager today; you can't tell me what to do. You're so old you probably don't even notice women anymore.* This kid will just flat out reject what you're offering.

2. Despairing: *I never get this right, and I never will.*

This teenager feels so convicted by the message, knowing that she failed so many times in the past despite her best intentions to do better. She wants to live right and honor God but has learned that in her own strength she'll only fall again. She doesn't realize she can grow and progress in her faith in ways that aren't fully dependent upon her own efforts and intentions. So she comes to the altar, cries, beats herself up, and then goes back to her seat sadder than she was before she responded to the altar call.

3. Determined: *I never get this right, but I will now.*

It's like Charlie Brown lining up to kick the football, as we cautiously root for him and halfway believe that maybe this time he'll get to kick it. This teenager gives us hope. He is readily responsive to the call to action and maybe even thanks you for sharing truth with him (imagine what that would feel like—a teenager actually thanking you for your sermon!). He leaves the service with a renewed determination to do better, to try harder, to get it right. But he's hoping in himself, not Christ.

4. Desensitized: *I never get this wrong.*

This teen has heard it all. She has sat through thousands of sermons and attended hundreds of youth events. She's pretty confident that her walk with Christ is much stronger than the others in the youth group. She's actually glad that you preached on gossip because she's hoping the others were listening. This student is on incredibly dangerous ground because she only thinks of sin in terms of behavior. I'll address this danger in more detail in the next chapter.

With each of these responses, the real problem here is that when a teenager listens to a moralistic sermon or a motivational talk, they leave with their minds and hearts focused on themselves—not on Jesus! They aren't stirred to gratitude and worship because Jesus was their substitute in life and death and because He is their source of positional righteousness and strength for behavioral righteousness. They are called to believe more in self-ability than in Christ's life, death, and resurrection. Behavior reveals our hearts. I believe that. But behavior is the fruit of our salvation, not the root of it.

If we're satisfied with measuring health by behavior, we're no different than a doctor who's satisfied by medicine that masks symptoms but does nothing to treat the sickness. The symptom is often behavioral issues, but the sickness lies in the heart. Moralism and motivationalism contain no real power to change the heart—only the gospel can do that. Look at how Paul makes this so clear in Colossians 2:20–23:

> Since you died with Christ to the basic principles of this world, why, as though you still belonged to it, do you submit to its rules: "Do not handle! Do not taste! Do not touch!"? These are all destined to perish with us, because they are based on human commands and teachings. Such regulations indeed have an appearance of wisdom, with their self-imposed worship, their false humility and their harsh treatment of the body, but they lack any value in restraining sensual indulgence.

Paul reminds the church that regulations and rules are attractive for many reasons, but they lack what our hearts need most: the power to realign the affections of our hearts. They can rein in our impulses and drive us to determination—and those aren't the worst things that could happen to us. But they can also lead us into spiritual pride, works righteousness, and an unhealthy reliance upon our rule-keeping abilities. "Do they behave?" isn't a bad question. It might serve us as a starting point for important conversations and ministry opportunities. But if we stop at that question we'll miss the opportunity to: (a) help the irreligious teenager recognize that his problem is much deeper than his behavior; and (b) protect the religious teenager from trusting in (placing saving faith in!) his own good behavior. There is much at stake.

I've learned something very telling about myself in those moments when I'm standing in the toy aisle, desperately pleading with one of my daughters to behave. What really motivates me to address her behavior with promises of ice cream and threats of "No Christmas!" are the looks that people give me when they walk by. In that moment, my validation as a good parent is at stake, and I would give anything for people to think I'm a good dad.

So the next time you see parents get ugly in public and yell at their kids, have sympathy for them, by all means—but also ask yourself, *Are they doing that because they love their kid, or because they love themselves?* For me, it's usually the latter.

I finish this chapter with that thought because if you're honest, one reason you want kids in your youth group to behave is because their good behavior and attendance at your events are sources of personal and ministerial validation. We say it's because we love them and want them to be lifelong followers of Christ, but we would do well to further examine our own hearts' motivations.

See how deep this goes when we focus on the question "Do they behave?" as a primary metric for health and our success? What hope do we have? Well, I'm glad you asked. On to the good news.

chapter three.

GOOD NEWS
VS. GOOD ADVICE

W hen I visit a great restaurant and it's time to order, it feels like torture to have to choose only one entrée. I want to sample everything! My forehead breaks out into beads of sweat as the server stares at me. I read and reread the descriptions of each dish as if they contain a secret code revealing which one's best. I like everyone else to order first so I can comfort myself with the thought that maybe one of them won't finish their entrée and I'll get to try it. One of the great things about having little girls is that they never finish their meals. It would be even greater if their taste buds evolved beyond a preference for pizza, hotdogs, chicken nuggets, and fries.

For this reason and many others, I love *tapas*, a.k.a. small plates. Tapas are most closely identified with Spanish cuisine—

plates of meats, cheeses, olives, and other finger foods. But tapas can also include smaller portions of entrée-type dishes. At a tapas restaurant, each person orders several tapas, and the group shares. It's wonderful. It's magical. It's glorious! The sound of the plates passing around the table must be what it sounds like when angels sing.

One night I was in downtown Philadelphia sitting with a couple of friends at a really fantastic tapas-style restaurant. I ordered the lamb chops, medium rare. When it comes to steak and lamb, I'm a rare to medium-rare guy. A quick public service announcement: If you prefer your steak well done, save yourself some money and order chicken. A well-done steak is a culinary crime.

So my perfectly cooked lamb came out, and I turned to one of my friends to begrudgingly ask him if he wanted to try some. His complete lack of excitement prompted me to ask him if he had ever actually eaten lamb before. He assured me that he was "pretty sure" he had. I didn't want to hand over any of my lamb, but I definitely wanted to sample his tapas. So as angry, hot tears of regret streamed down my face, I sliced off a large piece of my lamb and passed it to him. As he ate it, the look on his face changed from, *I hope this guy doesn't want to try any of my food,* to, *What have the gods just provided for my previously ignorant taste buds?* When he was done, he said, "You know I thought I had tasted it before, but now—I'm thinking I've never actually had real lamb before." The real thing exposed and eclipsed all the counterfeits.

I'm a pastor's kid. I attended a Christian high school. I was as involved with church activities and programs as anyone could be. I attended Bible school. I served in full-time local church ministry. I sat in more chapels, prayer meetings, and services than should be considered reasonable for one human being. Yet despite all that, there came a moment (or series of moments) in my adult life when I said to myself, I thought I knew what the gospel was before, but now—I'm thinking I've never actually understood and believed the real gospel before. The real thing exposed and eclipsed all the counterfeits. I'm deeply concerned that many young people think they have rejected Christianity when what they've really done is rejected a counterfeit (and rightfully so!). They've discovered and rejected the total uselessness of moralism and motivationalism that we talked about in chapter 2. They haven't ever really understood the gospel.

THE GOSPEL

So what's the gospel and how do we help students grasp the true gospel, not the counterfeit? Let's build some thoughts.

- The gospel is good news.
- The gospel is the good news about Jesus.
- The gospel is the good news about the person and work of Jesus.
- The gospel is the good news that God is rescuing sinners and restoring all of creation.

- The gospel is the good news that God is rescuing sinners and restoring all of creation through the person and work of Jesus.

The gospel is so rich and so deep that many different definitions can help us understand it. The gospel is the good news that Jesus accomplished for us what we could not accomplish for ourselves. It's the good news that the kingdom of God is here and coming. It's the good news that the very values of this world have been reversed. And the gospel is the good news that what God required, He provided.[1] The gospel is good news and not good advice.

Remember, moralism begins and ends with the message, "You can!" and motivationalism begins and ends with the message, "You should!" What about the gospel?

What our students need more than good advice is good news. And the best news is the gospel.

The gospel begins with the message: "You must! But you can't!" The human race owes God a perfect performance record. The only way a holy God can accept us is if we are perfect. The Ten Commandments set the bar high, and Jesus comes along many years later and raises the bar even higher— it's not just about behavior, it's about the heart (Matt. 5:21–30)! What hope do we have? How can we—sinful at birth and wicked in our hearts in ways we can't even understand—provide the righteousness required of us (Jer. 17:9)? We must, but we can't.

I'm so thankful the gospel doesn't end there but continues with this message: "Someone did! In Him, you can!" This is grace.

This is the love of a Father sending His Son to live in our place and to die in our place. We are called to respond in repentance and faith—to turn from all other forms of salvation and trust fully and solely in Jesus' work. This isn't a call to behave; it's a call to believe. Jesus taught that the Holy Spirit needed to convict us regarding our sin because we don't believe in Him—sin is a belief issue (John 16:8–9)! And the call to believe is grounded in the practice of beholding—remembering and rehearsing who God is and what He has done. What our students need more than good advice is good news. And the best news is the gospel.

If you have children, you know that one of the darker sides of having kids is that they end up embodying many of your faults and shortcomings. It's like looking into one of those distorted mirrors at some creepy carnival—it's a shorter version of you but the same basic makeup. One of the bad habits I've developed through life is biting my nails. (Hey, if God wanted us to use nail clippers, He wouldn't have given us perfectly functional nail clippers known as teeth.) So I bite my nails, but in moderation—for grooming purposes only. When our oldest daughter was four, my wife and I noticed she was biting her nails. (You can imagine the look my wife, who does not bite her nails, shot me.) But Lilia didn't do it in moderation; she would bite her nails until they bled. We needed to come up with a plan to motivate her to stop—apparently the bitter taste of her own blood wasn't doing the trick.

So my wife put together this little calendar that we hung on the wall. For every day that Lilia went without biting her nails (or being caught biting her nails), we put a sticker on the calendar. We told her that when she managed to go thirty days without biting her nails, we would buy her a toy. I know some of you are already judging our parenting approach. Well, it worked! She stopped biting her nails for a month, and we allowed her to pick out a toy. Note that I also agreed to stop biting my nails, and I did. I received no toy.

Pastor and author Tim Keller explains that one way to understand and process the word *righteousness* is "a validating performance record, which opens doors."[2] With our little reward strategy for Lilia, we had offered her a validating performance record opportunity that would open the door to a new toy. And it worked—Lilia changed her behavior, proved herself, and as a result had a new doll.

Here's the thing: Life is filled with one opportunity after another to validate ourselves through a performance record, all with the goal of opening some sort of door. Think about it. Report cards, physical fitness tests, attendance records, stars on a chart for bringing your Bible and offering to Sunday school, badges for church programs, athletic endeavors, and academic efforts. Ultimately, these performance trackers end up looking something like a transcript that opens the door to college, or a résumé that opens the door to employment. As an adult, these opportunities look like career success, family reputation, marital stability, church involvement, and more. They are all opportunities to validate ourselves through performances in an effort to open the doors to approval or security, or comfort or pleasure—you name it.

The gospel tells us that the very doors of true acceptance and approval are open to us now because of the performance record of Jesus!

Apart from the gospel, there's a total lack of assurance that we're both completely known and completely loved. Instead, we're left to our own pursuits and attempts to bring meaning into our lives. The gospel tells us that the very doors of true acceptance and approval are open to us now because of the performance record of Jesus! We don't have to exhaust ourselves trying in our own strength to manufacture righteousness or manage sin. We can receive, rest in, rejoice in, and respond to the righteousness of Jesus! That's the gospel!

FLUENT IN THE GOSPEL

Between 2004 and 2010, I had the opportunity to make five mission trips to the United Kingdom—three trips to Belfast, Northern Ireland, and two trips to Beaconsfield, England. As we prepared to reach teens, our teams quickly realized that if we were going to start conversations with the average UK teenager, we had to know something about soccer, specifically the English Premier League (EPL). So as part of our prep work to go to the UK, we spent time playing soccer, watching soccer, learning about the EPL, and picking favorite soccer teams. I lived in Liverpool, New York, so I decided to root for Liverpool FC. Very imaginative, I know.

Now I grew up feeling about soccer the same way most Americans feel about soccer. I totally didn't get it. First, there wasn't enough scoring to keep my attention. Spending ninety minutes of my life to watch a 1–0 final score made me want to kick something . . . or someone. Another issue was that soccer fans seemed okay with a tie. Sometimes they even called it a "good result" or a "fair result." To an American, there's nothing good or fair about not having a clear winner. Another problem I had with soccer was all the phantom injuries. Someone would get lightly bumped by a defender, and they'd drop to the ground rolling around like they were modeling "stop, drop, and roll," while screaming in pain like they had just been forced to watch a ninety-minute 0–0 soccer game. But my main issue with soccer was all the running. The only time I run is if I'm being chased— if you see me running, you should start running too. Running around non-stop just doesn't make sense to me.

So when we forced ourselves to learn about the EPL, the last thing I expected was to fall in love with soccer. But I did. Some of you may want to throw this book against the wall in protest at this point, but I'm now a bigger fan of the EPL than the NFL. Every Saturday morning I get up early to watch the matches, and I am now the one explaining to other people that in some cases, a draw is a fine result.

When I first started watching soccer, I had to make an intentional effort to use the right terms. Instead of saying "game," I reminded myself to say "match." When I was about to say "field," I would stop myself mentally and say "pitch." Even when it felt unnatural, I forced myself to use phrases like "good ball," "nice touch," and "that result was harsh."

I wasn't fluent in soccer terminology, and I had to learn. I still remember the moment when I knew I was finally "soccer (or football) fluent." I asked my friend where he planned to watch the "Dallas Cowboys-New York Giants match." He just shook his head and walked past me, slightly bumping into me in the process. I immediately dropped to the ground, grabbing at my ankle and rolling around.

If you're fluent in something, you think in it, you dream in it, you breathe it, you live it—basically, it becomes natural to you. It's your default mode. So what does it mean to be fluent in the gospel?

For much of my time in youth ministry, my default mode was to aim for behavior modification. When I would counsel a teenager who was struggling with a behavior, I would default to moralism. I would remind the young man that what he was doing was wrong and that it would hurt him and others in the process. I would encourage him to do the right thing and give him some biblical examples of people who did it right. Then I would let him know I would pray for him to make better choices in the future and offer accountability.

Because I wasn't fluent in the gospel, I didn't know how to help him identify the "sin beneath the sin," (more on that in the next steps section of chapter 3), and I didn't know how to join the Spirit's work in directing his wandering heart back to Jesus by reminding him of the gospel. I thought he needed a little instruction or a little inspiration when what he needed most was an invitation—an invitation to believe the gospel and the opportunity to grow in gospel fluency.

We need to cultivate gospel fluency in our lives and in the lives of our students because it's the gospel that captures our hearts, and it's the gospel that the Spirit uses to reveal Jesus to our hearts and minds.

TWO TENSIONS

At this point, I want to acknowledge and help us navigate a couple of tensions and important questions that some of the thoughts in this chapter may have introduced.

First, you might be thinking, *Can't the two motivations of fear and Jesus, and pride and the gospel, be used or leveraged for a student's good, to keep him on track?*

Second, you might be questioning, *If behavior isn't a primary indicator of health, does behavior matter? What about the need for right living? What about the fruit of the Spirit? What about a changed life? What about holiness?*

Can We Leverage Lesser Motivations? (Tension No. 1)

Let me talk about tension number one first. I would never say that lesser motivations of fear and pride couldn't be useful in our lives, especially in keeping us from making horrible decisions. Sometimes fear is useful and the desire to validate ourselves actually does keep us on the right track. But we have to pay careful attention to the motivations behind our actions because the same fear that motivates us to "be good" may someday motivate us to "be bad." For example, the fear of disappointing a youth pastor by not signing up for the student leadership team could someday lead a student to enslave himself to his studies and career. The drive for approval that keeps a teenager involved in youth group could be the same root that eventually causes her to jump into a destructive relationship.

When a student changes his behavior for any reason other than a growing love and appreciation for Jesus, the likelihood exists that he's worshiping another god—an idol. Let me explain. An idol is anything we treasure and trust in more than Jesus. Ironically, idols are usually good things that are elevated and made into ultimate things. In this context, Jesus (and church, youth group, and religious activities) becomes a means to an end. As I said in chapter 2: He's not a beautiful treasure, but rather a useful tool. He isn't what our hearts most desire; He helps us get what our hearts most desire, whether that's security, comfort, approval, or influence, etc. I believe one of the greatest dangers youth leaders face is the temptation to motivate (or manipulate) unconverted teenagers to behave like Christians. When we do that, we leverage the idols of their hearts instead of challenging these idols and exposing them as worthless.

> *I believe one of the greatest dangers youth leaders face is the temptation to motivate (or manipulate) unconverted teenagers to behave like Christians.*

It's worth noting that idolatry in the Old Testament wasn't always a case of Baal in place of Jehovah; often it was Baal in addition to Jehovah. The Israelites didn't flat out reject God. They hedged their bets. They said yes to God and yes to other gods, just in case. They didn't trust fully and solely in the God of Abraham, Isaac, and Jacob. As Scripture repeatedly drives home to us, we can't serve two gods. We can't expect students to make it in the long haul if their behavior is motivated by a mix of the gospel and self-preservation, or a mix of the gospel and self-justification.

But there is a uniquely Christian way to change—when we change what we worship. And make no mistake, everyone worships something or someone. In 2005, Pulitzer Prize-winning author, David Foster Wallace, gave the commencement address at Kenyon College. In his remarkable speech, he tapped into humans' unavoidable propensity to worship.

In the day-to-day trenches of adult life, there is actually no such thing as atheism. There is no such thing as not worshipping. Everybody worships. The only choice we get is what to worship. And an outstanding reason for choosing some sort of God or spiritual-type thing to worship . . . is that pretty much anything else you worship will eat you alive. If you worship money and things—if they are where you tap real meaning in life—then you will never have enough. Never feel you have enough. It's the truth. Worship your own body and beauty and sexual allure and you will always feel ugly, and when time and age start showing, you will die a million deaths before they finally plant you. . . . Worship power—you will feel weak and afraid, and you will need ever more power over others to keep the fear at bay. Worship your intellect, being seen as smart—you will end up feeling stupid, a fraud, always on the verge of being found out. And so on. Look, the insidious thing about these forms of worship is not that they're evil or sinful; it is that they are unconscious. They are default settings.[3]

I know what you're thinking: *Why am I reading this book instead of something by David Foster Wallace?* He hits it right on the head here. All of us are wired for worship—teenagers are no different. Whatever they worship determines how they live. And when we chase behavior without pointing to a God worth beholding, we short-circuit the way in which God wants to change them. Changing what we worship is how we change how we live.

Doesn't Behavior Matter? (Tension No. 2)

We can think about righteousness in the life of the believer in two different ways: positional righteousness and behavioral righteousness. Positional righteousness (right standing) is the immediate result of justification (the act by which repentant sinners are declared righteous by and before a holy God because of faith alone in the person and work of Jesus). In this sense, every Christian, regardless of maturity, is equally righteous. We don't deserve it, we don't earn it—salvation is all grace. But that's not the end of the story.

Behavioral righteousness (right living) is the ongoing result of sanctification (the process by which God's Word and His Spirit work in the life of the believer to create the fruit of the Spirit and tangible life change). This life change should happen within the setting of Christian community. Both right standing and right living must be parts of a Christian's life. But I want to be clear: No amount of right living earns us right standing (Rom. 3:20, Titus 3:4–7). As our hearts remember and rehearse what it cost to provide us with right standing, we respond with right living.

My daughters have been known to watch a cartoon or two. I know my name will be immediately removed from consideration for "Christian Daddy of the Year," but they like a certain show featuring a mouthy little sponge that wears square-shaped pants. One of the episodes they love is called "The Best Day Ever," in which SpongeBob determines to have the perfect day and to no one's surprise, things don't go his way. But at the end of the day he realizes that all the ups and downs of his day actually made it his "Best Day Ever."

As a Christian, what would your "best day ever" look like?

- Your radio alarm clock goes off in the morning and on comes your favorite worship song. You immediately sit up in bed, hands raised, eyes (still) closed, singing in perfect harmony.

- You jump in the shower and suddenly begin praying and weeping for the nations. Soon enough, you can't even tell the difference between the shower water and your tears.

- You make breakfast for your entire family, praying over every ingredient and every dish as you serve it to them. While they're wolfing down your perfectly cooked omelets, you take the time to wash their feet, drying them with your hair.

- As you drive to work, other drivers begin to cut you off in traffic and honk their horns. Instead of what you normally do with your hands, you point your open hand toward them, pray for them and bless them.

- You don't waste one moment of your workday by checking your Twitter, Pinterest, or Fantasy Football team. It's your most productive day ever, and it's all for God's glory!

- During lunch, you stand up on the table and preach the gospel until people begin to fall under deep conviction and everyone gets saved.

- On your drive home, you go out of your way to find every homeless person and give them money—and a tract of course!

- At dinner you break the bread for the family, and you're pretty sure it gets miraculously multiplied.

- You have a three-hour devotional with your family, and everyone ends up anointed in oil and "slain in the Spirit."

- You lay in bed reading your Bible until you can't keep your eyes open one more moment.

And as you fall asleep, your last thought is: "Best. Day. Ever." According to the prophet Isaiah, our human efforts of righteousness are like filthy rags (Isa. 64:6). The apostle Paul looked at all of his religious activity apart from Christ literally summarized it as a pile of crap (Phil. 3:8). Keep that image in your mind and imagine holding up your "best day ever" to God, hoping He's impressed with your goodness. It doesn't work that way. We can't convince God to accept us with our right living. Our only hope is to be accepted by God because of Jesus. We throw ourselves completely upon Jesus, trusting that He has thrown Himself completely upon us. In other words, we are found in Him, and His righteousness is found on us.

So behavioral righteousness matters because of positional righteousness. I suggest that a deepening awareness of, and appreciation for, our right standing is the motivation for our right living. Some might say that too much talk about grace leads to wrong living, but I don't believe that. Grace, rightly understood, is the most powerful force for heart change. Grace teaches us to say no (Titus 2:12). The kindness of God leads us to repentance (Rom. 2:4). In fact, grace places claims on our lives that no set of rules or moral code can ever simulate. Only a salvation that is truly free can require everything of us.

> *Only a salvation that is truly free can require everything of us.*

If we've contributed to our right standing with our right living, then God is limited in what He can ask of us—we've done our part! In a sense, God now owes us. But if salvation is truly a free gift, then our part is to spend the rest of our lives receiving the gospel into every area of our lives, allowing it to run rampant in our hearts, changing us from the inside out. At the cross, we move from the impossible burden of owing God everything to the improbable joy of owing God everything.

Working through these tensions gives us the foundational understanding we need to teach and model the true gospel and help students continue to live gospel-fluent in a culture where self-preservation and self-motivation are the driving factors behind how we live.

WHEN WE FORGET THE GOSPEL

I find it interesting that much of the writings found in the New Testament can be categorized as teaching the gospel to people who already knew it. I recently completed a semester in seminary where I studied the formative period of the church. It literally took seconds for the church to pervert and confuse the basic concepts of the gospel.

As freeing and as powerful as living gospel-fluent is, it doesn't take long for us to drift from the gospel. Soon, like the Israelites, we wander away, attracted by lesser gods. Living gospel-fluent requires daily intentionality. (One of the best books to help you do this is *New Morning Mercies: A Daily Gospel Devotional* by Paul David Tripp.) [4]

When we forget the gospel, we begin to preach some other sort of good news to our hearts. We begin treasuring or trusting in something or someone other than Jesus—and creating idols. Here are some clear indicators that you as a youth leader are doing that:

- If you treasure numerical success in youth ministry more than Jesus, then you'll drive home from youth group either flying high because of how amazing the service went, or in the depths of despair because only five kids showed up and two of them are yours.

- If you treasure being thought of as a great preacher more than Jesus, then on the day after a great sermon you'll repeatedly relive the best moments of your sermon in your head. But when things don't go well, you'll be miserable for days thinking about those kids in the back of the room who were more interested in choking each other than listening to your brilliantly exegeted, well-crafted talk.

- If you treasure creating emotional moments more than Jesus, then an altar full of crying teens validates your ministry. On the nights where there is a total lack of response—even from the one kid who always responds—you'll question your calling while drowning your feelings of ineffectiveness in a heaping bowl of ice cream.

- If you treasure the approval of students' parents more than Jesus, then you'll say yes to every idea and suggestion they have and try hard to make their kids happy.

- If you treasure control more than Jesus, then you'll never delegate responsibilities or trust other leaders with what matters most to you.

I'm not saying that surrounding circumstances don't affect us. We wouldn't be human if a great night at youth group didn't make us happy and if a really bad night didn't bum us out. But when the outcomes control your emotional stability and spiritual well-being, there's a real problem. There is a normal response to success and failure, and then there are responses that reveal we're forgetting the gospel. And when the gospel doesn't move us, we will add to or take away from it in an attempt to make it more interesting. Dried-up legalism and hyped-up mysticism look very different, but they share the same root: growing bored with the gospel.

I remember the day that some of my youth leaders mentioned in passing that I hated repeating myself. They told me that whenever I was asked to give instructions or information for a second time, there was always a different tone about it. I sounded annoyed, and I always responded with a shorter version. I didn't even realize I was doing this. But as I thought about it, I realized that there was a heart idol at work in these moments. Somewhere along the way I began to treasure being seen and respected as a gifted and clear communicator. When someone asked me to repeat something, it was as if they were calling into question my ability to communicate well. What I treasured was being threatened. And I responded through annoyance and frustration. Now that might seem like a harmless example, and of course it is. (Do you really think I'm going to share my harmful examples? But trust me—they are there.)

To foster a culture of gospel fluency, we must be fluent in the gospel ourselves. Being gospel-fluent starts with how we lead, why we lead, and the people we lead. If we're going to lead our groups and our students into gospel fluency, then we need to allow the Spirit to search our own hearts for the areas in which we're forgetting or ignoring the gospel. We need to focus on bringing the good news—not good advice. Let's look at practical ways to cultivate gospel fluency in our students.

next steps
CULTIVATING GOSPEL FLUENCY

*I*n these practical Next Step sections, you'll find proven ideas and tools. On the following pages, my hope is to offer specific ways to help you develop gospel fluency in your youth ministry— and as a result, in your students. You'll also get insights from a handful of local youth leaders whom I have asked to weigh in on these ideas and share how they practically approach cultivating gospel fluency in their students.

1. Deepen the definition of sin.

Whether you're teaching a class, leading a small group, preaching, or simply having a conversation with a teenager, the way you talk about sin matters. Most students think of sin only in terms of what they have done: Sin is when they lie, lust, or lose their temper. But talking about sin only as behavior is merely treating the symptoms, not the sickness. Sinful behavior is a problem, but even more than that, it's an indicator of the real problem. Remember: Beneath every *what* is a *why*.

When a student comes to you with a sin issue, spend some time doing the hard work of getting to the why by asking some of the following questions:

- Why do you think you did that?
- Why do you think other people do that?
- Why did you feel like that was your best option?
- What sort of thoughts went through your mind before you made that choice?
- What strong emotions were you feeling?
- Why do you think you were experiencing those emotions?
- What was happening in your heart during that moment?
- Can you think of any hopes or fears that might have motivated you to do that?

As students respond to these questions and begin to reveal the why beneath the what, be sure to listen for the lie. Beneath every *what* is a *why*, and beneath every *why* is a *lie*. When a student says he has a lying problem (the *what*)—and you begin to realize his fear is that people won't like him if they know the real person (the *why*)—then you can narrow in on the lie he is believing: The approval of people is worth more than the approval of God.

Students may not sense God's approval because they don't belong to Christ, or because they believe His acceptance comes and goes based on their goodness. In that case, they aren't resting and rejoicing in the goodness of Jesus. So essentially, the lie they believe is some combination of "God is not as gracious as the gospel reveals Him to be," and "God is not as good as the gospel says He is." (Author Tim Chester does an amazing job unpacking this truth in his book, *You Can Change*.)[1]

"Sin is preferring something other than God and acting on those preferences. We continually remind students that sin causes separation between each other and God."

—**Rob,** youth pastor

Once you've identified the lie, you can begin to speak the gospel into a student's heart and life. Remind her of who God is and the promises that He has made to His children. Help her see that Jesus spoke the truth even though it sent Him to the cross. But Jesus didn't just do that as an example—He did it as our substitute. Jesus never lied; and when we trust fully and solely in Him, His perfect record secures God's approval for us. Remind her that if we have to secure God's approval by always getting it right, then it's a vicious cycle of:

- Trying to do the right thing to get God's approval;
- Not being able to do the right thing because we can't overcome our need for the approval of others;

- Being enslaved to the approval of others because we don't sense God's approval;
- Not sensing God's approval because we don't always get it right.

Only the truth and the beauty of the gospel break this cycle. When Jesus instructed the woman caught in adultery to "Go and sin no more," it was on the heels of showing her undeserved and unexpected forgiveness and mercy. Jesus decided to eat in Zacchaeus' house before Zacchaeus committed to making restoration to those he had robbed. Only a heart-level encounter with grace truly changes the sinner. There is the sin beneath the sin. Help students look beneath the *what* to the *why* to the *lie*. And then point them to the truth of who God is and what He has done.

"If students don't have a clear grasp on their need for transformation, they'll see everything we teach as a means to gain self-righteousness rather than receiving Christ's."

—Jeremiah, youth pastor

"When a student shares how he wants to present a passage, I quickly can see if his view of the Bible is gospel-centered or moralistic; the good news or good advice; filled with heroes to worship or filled with men and women who point to the One True Hero. Once I assess where he is, I can coach him to gospel fluency as we craft a sermon together."

—Jim, youth pastor

2. Avoid preaching Jesus as . . .

I've heard many youth messages, and I don't think I've heard one that doesn't mention or reference Jesus at some point. Somehow, somewhere, at some point He gets an obligatory mention . . . even if it's just in the closing prayer.

But is that good enough?

I've witnessed four ways that Jesus is often preached to teenagers.

Admittedly, I've done these too many times. Maybe you have too.

Jesus as an Inspirational Example

The main idea: Jesus did it; you can do it!

The problem: This approach appeals to a student who measures his worth in terms of accomplishment, spiritual or otherwise. It works on the will but not the heart. If Jesus is only an example, then the average teenager is in a lot of trouble because, well, Jesus was perfect. Your teenagers need much more than an example to inspire them (or eventually crush them). They need a Savior to rescue them.

The result: You might get teenagers to change their behavior, but it will be in their own strength and with a hint of moralism. This isn't the gospel. Jesus didn't die on the cross to give us a second chance to get things right. He did it because He knew we never would.

"I always ask myself 'Could I give this talk at a public school assembly by simply trading out some illustrations and get to the same application?' If my answer is yes, more often than not I'm preaching moralism."

—**Jeremiah**

Jesus as a Faithful Sidekick

The main idea: Jesus did it, and He will help you do it!

The problem: This approach reduces Jesus from the central character of the story of our salvation to the silent partner who simply helps us live right. He becomes nothing more than the greatest tool in your toolbox. One more metaphor: Jesus gets the assist, but I get the goal. The gospel is not that He helps us get it right, but that He got it right in our place. Big difference.

The result: You may get teenagers fired up, but you may also make them self-reliant, filled with unhealthy expectations. If they think that all they need is a boost from their buddy Jesus to be okay, then they may not understand the depth of their own depravity. Grasping, on a profound level, how lost we are becomes the starting point to encountering Jesus.

Jesus as a Jilted Boyfriend/Girlfriend

The main idea: Jesus did it for you, so don't hurt His feelings and let Him down!

The problem: This approach appeals to students' emotions, fears, and sense of guilt. Most people don't want to disappoint or let down anyone, let alone God!

But as I wrote about in chapter 3, fear and guilt are not gospel motivations; they're tools of the Enemy.

The result: You may get emotionally driven responses, especially from students who want to please people. They'll make all sorts of radical promises about "never ever, ever sinning again." However, teenagers will eventually find someone else (peers, boyfriend, girlfriend . . .) whom they don't want to disappoint even more than God. That relationship will easily trump this type of change.

Jesus as a Divine Loophole

The main idea: Jesus did it, and you should too. But if you don't, He'll forgive you!

The problem: This approach can be combined with any of the previous three. It weakens the message of the gospel and the power of grace. Either the grace of God is the most powerful change force for mankind, or we're hopeless. The "get-out-of-jail-free card" approach to grace doesn't communicate that.

The result: Some teenagers will come to see Jesus as nothing more than the great eraser. They do whatever they want and come to Him, hoping He can hit the reset button for them. It makes them feel better, but it doesn't invite them into the story of the gospel. Eventually, they won't believe it; they'll believe they've fallen too far. Or they just won't be drawn to a grace that's strong enough to forgive them when their hearts wander, but too weak to truly win their affections.

3. Preach Jesus from All of Scripture.

The Old Testament is filled with great stories that reveal much about human nature and the workings of God. But framing those stories within the full story of Scripture is crucial. If we remove Old Testament narratives from the metanarrative of Scripture, then we'll be prone to moralize or allegorize those stories.

"Being a great preacher is about more than keeping people's attention. Ultimately it's about showing them that the whole Bible is about the person and work of Jesus Christ."

—**Matt,** youth director

A classic example of how to preach Jesus from the Old Testament is the story of David and Goliath. (I've heard several different speakers give the following example.) We tend to make David and Goliath about ourselves—how can we defeat the giants in our lives, and have the courage and bravery, and trust in God to go and do great things on the battlefield of life? That's a fine challenge, but when we take a step back and see this story in the light of the gospel, we realize that we're not David. Instead, we're the Israelites: afraid, doubting, unable, and unwilling to bring about the victory the people need. So God sends an unexpected hero who goes out and wins the battle in our place. His victory becomes our victory even though we didn't fight, and the spoils of the battle are ours as well. Seeing Jesus as our substitute who defeated the giants of death, sin, and shame empowers us to face the giants in our lives. (If you want a crash course in learning to see the Bible this way, check out *The Jesus Storybook Bible* by Sally Lloyd Jones.[2])

"Learning to preach Christ in all of Scripture brought clarity to the full narrative of Scripture for the first time in my life. It was so eye-opening. While this takes time, study, and work, it opens up the Scriptures and brings unparalleled clarity."

—**Justin,** former youth pastor, now college campus minister

"To preach this way—and do it well—I have to do my homework: get into the text, chew on it, and cross-reference with commentaries. It takes solid study, but when a listener has an 'aha' moment and realizes all of the Bible whispers the name of Jesus, there's nothing like it in the world."

—**Jeremiah**

All of Scripture points to Jesus. On the road to Emmaus as Jesus walked with two disciples after His resurrection, He did something remarkable: "Beginning with Moses and all the prophets, Jesus explained to them what was said in all of the scriptures concerning himself" (Luke 24:27). All of Scripture is either preparation for, anticipation of, presentation of, application of, or the implications of—the gospel!

"Allowing the message of the gospel to be the end point of every study or teaching allows students to see that the gospel isn't just the start of our faith; it's the beginning, end, and everything in

between. Ultimately, this framework becomes the starting point by which they view the world."

—**Stephanie,** youth worker

4. Avoid the "Sucker's Choice."

In their insightful book *Crucial Conversations: Tools for Talking When Stakes Are High,* authors Kerry Patterson and Joseph Grenny write about avoiding "the sucker's choice." [3] In short, "the sucker's choice" is when we force an "either/or " dilemma when it can actually be a "both/and" opportunity. You may have heard someone say something like: "Either we can have fun or we can have competition," implying that you can't possibly find a way to have both fun and competition. Forcing the either/or sets up an unnecessary ultimatum, aptly named "the sucker's choice."

In youth ministry, we often make "the sucker's choice" when we preach. Either we prepare and deliver a message with non-Christian teenagers in mind, or we prepare and deliver a message with Christian teenagers in mind. We don't have to make that choice. There's a way to effectively preach to both audiences at the same time and with the same words—preach the gospel.

I remember a time when I thought the gospel message was only for those who didn't know Christ. I thought that, in time, mature believers "graduated from the gospel." I was so wrong. The message of the gospel is our faithful companion every step of the way. We never graduate from the truth of the gospel. Rather, we cling to it and allow it to bring about increasing change in our lives.

The Christian way to drive out lesser loves (idols) is to center our lives daily on our greatest affection. Nineteenth-century theologian Thomas Chalmers said it this way: "We know of no other way by which to keep the love of the world out of our hearts than to keep in our hearts the love of God."[4] Like I said earlier, we are prone to sin when we believe a lie about the nature of God. The gospel is the most intimate and intensive reminder of who God is and what He has done. We need to be gospel-fluent with students, with our families, and with ourselves!

"The more clearly we see the same heart idols at work in both Christians and non-Christians, the more we'll be able to preach beyond particular behaviors and press into the same heart conditions both types of people can relate to."

—Rob

There's one final reason to avoid "the sucker's choice" (I learned this gem also from Tim Keller).[5] Christian teenagers need to hear you talking to non-Christian teenagers, and non-Christian teenagers need to hear you talking to Christian teenagers about the gospel. As you preach the gospel in a way that engages and answers the questions and objections of the irreligious, Christian teenagers will learn how to do the same! Those same students will also realize that youth group is a place to bring their non-Christian friends to get their questions answered.

On the other hand, non-Christian teenagers need to hear you talking to Christian teenagers about the gospel because they need a sense of the community, the values, the priorities, and the passion of a Christ-like people—and the *reason* for them, which is the gospel. They also need to experience a growing sense that they are on the outside of something beautiful, namely Jesus.

In Romans 1:15, Paul writes that he is "eager to preach the gospel." Don't miss that he's writing to Christians! There's no need to make "the sucker's choice." Preach the gospel to the lost; preach the gospel to the found.

"Christian and non-Christian students need the continual reminder of the gospel message because the human heart will always seek to drift away from it toward self-righteousness or despair."

—Matt

5. Celebrate Communion and Water Baptism.

Most youth groups I've been around don't make communion a regular part of their gathering. This is a mistake. Communion is a tangible way for your students to celebrate and reflect upon the cross. It's experiential and engaging without feeling forced or unusual—most students have taken communion at some point in their lives and won't be scared off by it. Think of creative ways to celebrate communion and consider making it a regular part of your youth service. Be sure to take the time to carefully and clearly explain the symbolism of the Lord's Table and its elements.

Water baptism also offers a beautiful and symbolic way to share the gospel. If students are responding to the gospel in your youth ministry, then make it a normal next step to get baptized in water. You can invite parents to join (you certainly may want to get their approval). If your teenagers are water-baptized in the adult service, then consider filming those baptisms and editing them into a highlight video to show your youth group. Once again, always explain the meaning of the ceremony.

"Often, if there are youth who don't actively attend the main services (which is common for us), they might never experience communion and water baptism. Yet, these sacraments are fundamental in understanding the union we have with Christ and one another in community. If we want healthy gospel community, we must have communion and baptism."

—Justin

"Celebrating communion with students is one of the greatest teaching tools to move them beyond the 'me' of salvation toward the 'us' of authentic biblical community."

—Matt

6. Help Students Understand Their Own Faith Story.

One way to evaluate the level of gospel fluency in your youth group is to ask core kids to share their faith story with you. In preparations for mission trips, we always asked our students to come up with a two- to three-minute version of their faith story. Almost without fail, the first time through sounded something like this:

> "Well, I was raised in a Christian home so I've always been around church and God and stuff. But I really

was struggling with owning my faith, and then I went to this amazing youth retreat and the speaker said something (I don't even really remember what he said), and I realized I needed to get serious with my faith. So I started going to youth group more regularly, and I stopped doing some bad things, and now I'm doing great!"

What's missing? Well, Jesus for one. That story sounds like the teenager saved himself. When teenagers tell their faith story, Jesus is often missing in action. He's rarely the hero of their story. Helping students reconsider their faith story (ask, "Where is Jesus in your story?" and "How is He the hero?") is part of the process of growing in gospel fluency. When a teenager finishes sharing her faith story, the listener should be more impressed with Jesus than with the teenager.

"For students to know their story, they must first see the larger story God is telling: creation > fall > redemption > restoration. The more students see God's bigger story that He's inviting them into, the more compelled they will be to see how their story partners with the gospel."

—Rob

"Something profound happens in the minds of students when they realize that their salvation is primarily for God's own glory. When they view what they have been given in Christ as something they steward, rather than something they own, it increases the way they value the gospel at work in them."

—Matt

7. *Expect the Visitor and Explain the* Why.

Our youth service usually followed a predictable order:

1. Welcome

2. Announcements

3. Mixer/game

4. Prayer element

5. Singing time—usually three songs

6. Sermon

7. Response/closing

8. Praying that parents would come pick up their teenager on time!

I remember a night when we had a lot of visitors. After the service, I went up to a group of the guys and thanked them for coming out. The conversation went something like this:

> *Me:* "Hope you guys had a good time here—I'd love to hear your thoughts."
> *Them:* "Yeah, man—we did. You're the best speaker we've ever heard. Because of how you handled that text and masterfully applied it to our lives, I think we'll never be the same. We can't wait to give all our money to this church."
> *Me:* "Sounds about right."
> Okay, that didn't happen. Ever. Let me try again.

Me: "Hope you guys had a good time here—I'd love to hear your thoughts."

Them: "Yeah, it was cool. We liked the music."

Me: "That's great! The band works really hard to get ready for Wednesday nights."

Them: "Yeah, they were pretty good. But that was a really long song."

Me: "Long song? Which one?"

Them: "What do you mean which one?"

Me: [realizing they didn't know it was three different songs]

We are so used to how church works that sometimes we lose sight of how outsiders see things. Our "Christianese" and our insider talk can be real obstacles to the gospel. One way to be gospel-fluent is to be intentional in the language we use. As you prepare, ask yourself helpful questions: "Will this make any sense to someone who has never been in church before?" "How can I say this in a more simple and accessible way?" "Will this create confusion or clarity in the mind of a biblically illiterate teenager?"

Also, be sure to take thirty to sixty seconds in every service to bring the gospel into focus by explaining why you do certain things: giving, singing, preaching, praying, etc. Explaining the "why" provides a valuable opportunity to put visitors at ease and lets them know you're expecting and considering them while also teaching your church kids the why—trust me, many of them don't know!

Two quick examples:

- "Hey everyone, we're going to stand now and sing a few songs together. The reason we sing is because singing is just one way that we tell God how we feel about Him and how we remind ourselves of who God is and what He's done for us."

- "Hey friends, at this time in the night, we give you all the opportunity to honor God and respond to His generosity to you by giving of your hard-earned money. This is just one small way we tell God that all we have belongs to Him because He gave everything to save us. The Bible tells us that Jesus, who was rich, became poor for us and died in our place so that we could be given the riches of God's love."

Expect the visitor and explain the *why*.

"In our weekly service, I would welcome visitors from the stage and take a few minutes to say who we were and what we were about, using the same key words that defined our mission and values. This helped put first-time guests at ease and reinforced the mission for those who were there every week."

—Matt

"If I'm not preparing for and expecting visitors, I'll inevitably make them feel like outsiders when they do come and ensure

they don't return. If I'm preparing for visitors (even if they're not present), I'm communicating to everyone present that this would be a good place to bring someone who is curious about God, faith, Jesus, etc."

—Jeremiah

8. Pay Attention to the Songs Your Group Sings.

When a youth event is over, the students don't usually leave quoting the speaker (unless he or she makes a Freudian slip on stage), but they do leave singing the songs. They won't download podcasts of the speaker, but they'll download the album of the band. My point is obvious. Music is powerful, and the lyrics to the songs our students sing matter. I once sat in a service where they sang for forty-five minutes and not once did they sing the name of Jesus. Oh, we sang about rain and fire and wind and rivers and oil, but not Jesus. I see a couple of problems with this.

First, many of your students are pretty much concrete thinkers only. So when you're singing about fire, as some metaphor for what God wants to do, they're thinking about real fire. When you sing about rain, they're thinking about umbrellas. When you sing about a river, they need to go to the bathroom. I get that there are metaphors for the Holy Spirit and the workings of God in the Bible. I get that poetic language can be beautiful and powerful. But I also believe that singing the clear message of the gospel is one of the best things a youth group can do to create gospel fluency. I like to sing songs that so clearly point to the character of God and/or the person and work of Jesus that someone could get converted while singing them.

"I can't emphasize enough the importance of Christ-centered preaching working in tandem with Christ-centered singing. Worship leaders should be in full communication with preaching pastors to not only plan for content alignment, but to help deliver a cohesive and redemptive message that's worth gathering around."

—**Jonathan,** worship pastor

In youth ministry, there's a tendency to choose songs that are catchy, musically edgy, and current. That's fine, but there should be additional filters and considerations. We should be singing about God more than we sing about ourselves. We should be choosing songs that are God-exalting and Christ-centered and are not riddled with cryptic insider language that makes it sound like we're at a pep rally for pyromaniacs or worshippers of the elements of the earth.

"We ask two questions about every song before we choose to sing it corporately: Is the primary focus of this song celebrating God's character? Is the primary focus of this song celebrating the person and work of Jesus?"

—**Rob**

Imagine a kid sitting in her house later that night, singing the song she learned at youth group. Wouldn't it be great if the lyrics in that song were actually cultivating gospel fluency in her? I think so.

"This is so necessary and yet so difficult. Every song is preaching a sermon, and it must align with the values of Christ. Yet, it's

difficult because the most popular, catchy, or thought-provoking songs may be quite 'me-centered' or theologically anemic. It can often be a battle that needs to be fought with love and grace."

—Justin

9. Offer the Good News, Not Good Advice.

You're in youth ministry because you want to help kids. You want to see teenagers do well and avoid the mistakes you made. And so you give advice—a lot of it. And advice can be useful, but gospel fluency isn't about good advice. It's about the good news. Listen to your sermons, your small group discussions, and your conversations with teenagers. Are they more about good advice or the good news? Here are some distinguishing characteristics:

Good advice inspires us to finish well.
The good news assures us that it is finished.

Good advice is about what you must do.
The good news is about what has been done for you.

Good advice shapes your mind.
The good news shapes your heart.

Good advice can change how you live.
The good news will change how you love—which, in turn, changes how you live.

Good advice assists you in the pursuit of approval and acceptance.

The good news establishes you as approved and accepted before God—not on the basis of your performance record, but on the basis of another's.

Good advice requires you to achieve something.
The good news invites you to receive something.

"The good news of Jesus causes a shift in our focus from someone's behavior to his heart. When the gospel is the foundation, our trust is in the person and work of Christ as the One who brings life and changes hearts."

—**Krista,** volunteer youth worker

"It's hard not to give advice because I want to be the answer to their problem. My desire to be the hero can get in the way of them seeing the true hero. As long as I'm giving advice, I'm reproducing disciples of me."

—**Jeremiah**

We're not called to be dispensers of good advice. We're called to be the ones who declare and demonstrate the good news. And there's a big difference.

On February 11, 2014, our third daughter was born. She came into the world three months early, weighing slightly more than two pounds. She had suffered a significant brain injury in utero, and the doctors had prepared us for the worst. My wife

Erin and I went into the emergency room for the Cesarean delivery not knowing if we would leave the room with a living, breathing child. I'll never forget the moments when Madelaine first entered the world. She was immediately rushed over to a warming table and surrounded by nurses and doctors. I stared at the scene, waiting for any sign of hope and health. The doctor began telling us bits and pieces of information: "She's pinking up . . . she's breathing . . . her head doesn't look deformed . . ." Then they whisked her up to the neonatal intensive care unit where she spent the next seventy-nine days of her life.

Four days after her birth, I held Madelaine for the first time. At that point, she weighed less than two pounds and had to be held "kangaroo style," tucked into my shirt, skin on skin—her head resting on my chest, just below my neck. And as I held her praying and thanking God for His plans for her, I began to sing quietly to her and to myself:

> *"How deep the Father's love for us,*
> *How vast beyond all measure*
> *That He would give His only Son*
> *To make a wretch His treasure."[6]*

On some of the darkest days of my life, I didn't need good advice. I needed the good news. Without the gospel, you'll never succeed well, and you'll never suffer well. The gospel reminds us that we can boast only in our weaknesses and in Christ. Even our moments of success point us to Jesus.

But the gospel also assures our hearts that every good thing in our lives is because of the grace of God. When a legalist/

moralist suffers, he'll be angry at God (for not holding up His end of the bargain) or at himself (for not holding up his end of the bargain). When gospel-fluent Christians suffer, they understand that since it's all grace, there's nothing God can't ask of them. He owes us nothing, but gave us everything.

My prayer is that you will begin or continue the journey to gospel fluency in your own life and in the lives of the students you lead—young men and women who will encounter many days where they desperately need the good news.

Big Events

chapter four.

CRY ME A RIVER

*I*t was the last day of another successful winter retreat and time to head home. I was sitting in the church van reflecting upon another year of great services, successful community building, and the miracle of no injuries on the tubing hill. My thoughts were interrupted when a teenager opened the passenger-side front door and took the seat next to me. As we began the two-hour drive home, I asked him what he thought about the weekend. We began to discuss the guest speaker's messages, the mysterious smells in his room, and the even more mysterious meat we all ate the previous night.

In the middle of the conversation, he turned to me and said, "This was a good year, but last year's retreat was better." Naturally, I was intrigued. "Why?" I asked him. His reply was telling.

"I cried more last year," he said.

Now before you accuse me of being a heartless Grinch-like monster whose heart is shriveled up like a prune and half the size it should be, let me confess something: I'm a crier. I'm a naturally emotional person, and it doesn't take a lot for me to get weepy. A well-done commercial set to the right song can make me a little bit teary, especially if it shows a perfectly cooked piece of steak I'll never get to taste. Many movies have moved me to tears—like *Saving Private Ryan, The War,* and *Rocky 3* (that's not a joke—Mickey's death was rough on this tender soul). I also become emotional watching sporting events. I love watching underdogs battle against the odds.

I still remember the day. It was October 26, 1996. The New York Yankees were a game away from winning their first World Series in nearly two decades and completing a comeback from being down two games to none—and this eighteen-year-old die-hard Yankees fan had to work. I wasn't a happy camper.

I was listening to the drama unfold on a small radio in the full-service gas station where I worked. When Charlie Hayes caught the foul ball pop-up for the final out of the 1996 World Series, I exploded into motion. I began running in circles around this little gas station while screaming and giving high-fives to my invisible friends. Then I collapsed into a metal folding chair, put my head in my hands . . . and cried.

I'm also the type of person who cries when I really sense God working in me. I can barely preach the gospel without getting emotional. When I think about Hosea walking into a sex-slave market to buy back Gomer, I want to cry. When I imagine the father running to the prodigal son and pleading with the older son, I want to cry. The gospel moves me!

I say all that to say this: I'm not against crying or emotions, and I'm certainly not against expressing emotions in church. I serve in a Pentecostal stream of Christianity. A Pentecostal against emotions is a bit of an oxymoron. But I am concerned about emotional experiences and hyped-up events being a primary indicator of healthy youth ministry. To reiterate, I'm not anti-crying. I'm anti-measuring impact based solely on how many tears I can crank out of a group of teenagers.

When that young man explained to me what made the difference between the two retreats, it hit me smack in the face. Many teenagers evaluate spiritual growth and the work of the Spirit based solely on how they felt during the service. You've probably heard these comments from teenagers in your youth group about the last big event they attended:

"The speaker was so funny—he made me laugh a lot."
"The band was so amazing—I loved the drummer!"
"There's nothing like singing with so many other teenagers!"
"The videos they showed were so cool!"
"The energy in the room was incredible!"
"I've never experienced anything like that."
"I wish I could stay there."
"I cried a lot."
"I had a real moment."
"I know that I have to make some changes."
"I really felt good."

Most teenagers don't connect the impact of an event with a characteristic of God that they now better understand.

What you probably won't hear are comments describing a new or growing appreciation for Jesus or an increased awareness of the nearness of the Spirit. Most teenagers don't connect the impact of an event with a characteristic of God that they now better understand.

I know that most teenagers don't naturally think or talk in those terms, but that's the point. Shouldn't we be working to help form and shape the way students think and talk about spirituality? When we continue to offer an onslaught of big events, have we somehow bowed the knee to consumerism and hype, refusing to challenge and expose the potential dangers in those things?

THE NEXT BIG EXPERIENCE

Clearly, the rampant consumerism of our society has made its way into the church. Many churchgoers choose their church based on how it meets their needs: Where can they hear the best teaching? Who has the best music? Who has the programs perfectly tailored to their family? Which church produces the best weekend experience?

Each week, they show up to consume spiritual goods, evaluating them as they walk out the door: "Hmm. The band seemed a little off their game today"; or, "Pastor Jack shared some hilarious stories in his message"; or, "It felt a little chilly in the sanctuary today—can't they control that?" Because we have unprecedented access to countless options in every arena of life, we expect to be accommodated and considered as consumers . . . even at church. I just did a quick search on Amazon for "garden hose": 23,948 results! Who needs that many options for something that will end up run over by the lawn mower in a couple of weeks?

Being the dad to three little girls means that my life as a grown man is much different than I ever imagined it would be. I often describe my life as "dolls, drama, and Disney." We have enough princess dolls to fill a castle. Disney's toy producers and marketers are geniuses—they don't just sell one version of the latest Disney princess; they come up with multiple dolls. I just searched Amazon for "Rapunzel doll" (I couldn't help myself): 796 results. Who needs 800 different types of the same doll? My daughters. That's who. (By the way, my Amazon search history looks odd right now.)

So when my family ends up in the local Disney store (a.k.a. the fifth chamber of hades), I end up having the same exact conversation with one of my daughters:

Them: "Daddy! Look at these Belle dolls!"
Me: "That's great, sweetie. They sure look a lot like the other five Belles you have at home."
Them: "No, this one has bigger eyes!"
Me: "As someone who is Asian, you should know that's no advantage in life."
Them: "And this one has real hair."
Me: "Creepy."

Them: "But this is the one I really want! This one . . .
can go in water!!"
Me: "Baby, as far as I'm concerned, all of your dolls can
go in water. Preferably a moving body of water—like a
rushing river or a waterfall."
Them: "So does that mean I can get her?"
Me: . . .

Not once has one of my daughters looked at a variation of
a doll and said to me, "You know what? I don't need her. She's
actually quite similar to the other ones I have." Nope. Never.
Doesn't happen. Won't happen. Because they always need and
want *more.* What they have doesn't satisfy. What they don't have
captures their minds and hearts. They are relentless consumers,
and the geniuses of Disney merchandise are enabling them.

I think it's possible the big events that youth ministry has
become known for are actually partially responsible for creating
a form of youth spirituality that is fatally dependent on the
next "high." Every high has to be greater than the previous one.
Every retreat has to compete with the previous one and deliver
an experience that both entertains and engages a consumer
audience that becomes increasingly hard to entertain or engage.
It's difficult enough just to be more interesting than the phone
in their hand. So we ramp up our events to keep stringing them
along from a conference to a camp to a retreat, and repeat ad
nauseam. Except for the fact that eventually there is no next
event—they graduate from youth group, and now they have to live
out their faith without the promise of the next big experience.

On the local church level, it's easy for youth workers to get sucked into this same vortex of consumerism, providing bigger and better draws every week. At a youth workers' training session, I heard youth ministry veteran Duffy Robbins say, "What you win them with, you win them to." So if the promise of pizza is the main reason they come to youth group, then you have to keep providing that sort of draw to keep them coming. Eventually, you have to add chicken wings to the menu. If last week's game involved teenagers cramming dog biscuits dipped in raw egg into their mouths, then this week's game has to be even more disgusting.

> *On the local church level, it's easy for youth workers to get sucked into this same vortex of consumerism, providing bigger and better draws every week.*

It becomes exhausting to have to deliver these experiences, each one better than the last. We become like the man with the spinning plates, running from plate to plate trying to keep them all spinning, and hoping that if we can deliver the right experience at the right event, then we can know we've been successful and have a healthy youth ministry.

PREACHING IMPACT

Trying to deliver a better experience week in and week out also can affect the way you preach, how long you preach, and what you preach about. You might feel the pressure to be as engaging as Judah Smith or as funny as Reggie Dabbs or as handsome as Doug Fields. (I had to give my buddy Doug a shout out for writing the foreword of this book!) Instead of discovering and developing your own voice and style as a preacher, you mimic one of those guys—or the youth pastor across town with the huge youth ministry. But in doing so, you rob yourself of the opportunity to grow in your own unique way, and you rob your teenagers of the opportunity to hear from the real you.

If we're obsessed with trying to keep students entertained, then we might find ourselves cutting back our sermon time, especially if we know we aren't a very entertaining speaker. We end up going from a traditional youth talk to a TED talk to a Tweet. The youth leader stands up there, delivers 140 characters of solid biblical truth, says amen, and then yells, "Now who wants to cram something more disgusting than dog biscuits covered in runny egg yolk into their mouth?"

The other thing that can happen is the content of our preaching becomes determined by whatever is hot in culture at that time. We figure being culturally relevant means talking about whatever is the center of the pop culture world that week. So we go from a series entitled "Twerking: The Dance of the Devil" to a series called "Selfie: If God Wanted You to Have Duck Lips, He Would Have Made You A Duck!" In this case, the sermons aren't determined by timeless values, but instead are driven by temporary issues or trends.

UNSUSTAINABLE MOMENTUM

Every youth worker has experienced the frustration of coming off of a big event and being unable to sustain the energy and momentum. Youth group kids who seemed to make giant leaps in their faith in one weekend suddenly look very similar to who they were before the event. Some are able to maintain the impact a little longer, but soon enough the group moves from the nostalgia of the last event to the anticipation of the next one.

Many Christian teenagers would express their spiritual life as a roller coaster—up high during the big events and down low the rest of their lives. I've stood on stage at the end of big events and challenged students to not let the weekend be just an experience, to bring it home with them and make it a part of their everyday lives. But at home without the band, the speaker, and the environment, they can't sustain the moment.

A SPIRITUAL HIGHLIGHT REEL

Most teenagers don't really understand that God desires to be a part of even the seemingly mundane moments of their lives. It's difficult to grasp that when the way we read and teach the Bible highlights the milestone moments. The Bible, especially the Old Testament, is really the highlight reel version of these characters' lives. For example, Moses kills an Egyptian and has to run for his life. Next thing, God shows up in a burning bush to tell him to go back to Egypt and deliver His people. It seems like there's never a dull moment in Moses' life. But hold on—there were *forty* years between those two events! Forty years of getting up every day, living in the middle of nowhere, and walking around the desert with a bunch of sheep. If that isn't the definition of mundane, I don't know what is. Did God forget about Moses during those forty years? Was He a part of each of those days?

Sometimes we create a highlight-reel form of spirituality in youth ministry. Students develop an event-based spirituality; they're convinced that the lights must go down, the stage lights must go up, and the band has to hit the first chord before God will show up on the scene to meet with His people. But the halls of high school, their workplace, or their bedroom offer none of those indicators that God is there. At that point, we're feeding students' misperceptions of who the Holy Spirit is and how He works in their lives.

MISPERCEPTIONS AND LASTING FRUIT

Growing up in a Pentecostal church (for which I am very thankful!), I developed some misconceptions of the person and work of the Holy Spirit. I thought that God the Father was the old guy sitting up in heaven, God the Son was the nice guy who died on a cross for me, and God the Holy Spirit was the weird one. When anything weird or unusual happened in church, everyone credited (or blamed!) the Holy Spirit. It also seemed to me that the Holy Spirit only showed up at the end of the service, during the response time and specifically at the altar. It was like He was limited to specific times and places, but when those times and places aligned perfectly—watch out! Whenever the Holy Spirit showed up, things got loud, intense, weird, or some combination of the three.

There's a really interesting account in 1 Kings 18. Elijah had challenged the prophets of Baal to a worship battle—a worship throw-down of sorts. Baal's prophets would worship their god, and Elijah would worship Jehovah. The worshipper whose god sent fire to consume the offering on the altar would be declared the winner. This is like a reality TV competition way before its time. So the false prophets got to go first. They set up the altar, and their worship service began. It was quite a scene. They were loud and passionate and intense, carrying on with all sorts of energy, even cutting themselves with hopes that the spilt blood would draw the attention of Baal.

Nothing happened, and then up stepped Elijah. He wasn't nearly as outwardly passionate or worked up. He was actually quite normal—or at least as normal as you can be in a situation this odd. He prayed a simple prayer, and the fire fell. It consumed not only the offering, but also the entire altar and all the water that had been poured over it. The Israelites who watched all this happen fell to the ground crying out, "The LORD—He is God! The LORD—He is God!"

> *The strength of our worship is not found in how we worship, but in whom we worship.*

Note two things in this text. First, the strength of our worship is not found in *how* we worship, but in *whom* we worship. The value of the time spent singing in youth services is determined by how effective the songs and band are in helping focus the hearts of the teenagers toward Jesus—and not by the volume in the room, the lighting on the stage, the cutting-edge nature of the songs, or even the excellence of the band. I'm not against any of those things. Excellence in particular is a worthwhile value—we should be stewarding well the gifts of God, and excellence is a language everyone understands. But what makes our musical expression of worship more like Elijah's than the prophets of Baal's is who we worship, not how we worship.

> *When we tell ourselves that success and health in youth ministry mean delivering high-energy emotional moments, we run the risk of manipulating kids' emotions to get them to feel something.*

This story doesn't teach us that passion, intensity, and increased volume are always indicators of false worship. That's not it at all. But there is something worth considering. Whenever we use increased volume or emotion to (a) prove our level of devotion, or (b) try to manipulate divine activity, we're more like the prophets of Baal than Elijah. Think about it. The false prophets got crazy because they were trying to show how devoted they were, hoping their level of devotion and commitment would make their god answer their prayers. Their worship displayed a complete lack of confidence in their relationship with the god they worshipped. They didn't really know if he was reliable or if he would pay attention—they had to go to extreme measures to make sure he woke up, came back from vacation, or got off the toilet.

When we tell ourselves that success and health in youth ministry mean delivering high-energy emotional moments, we run the risk of manipulating kids' emotions to get them to feel something. And like Baal's prophets, we show a real lack of reliance upon the Spirit. It's like we don't trust that He will do His part so we're going to help fast-track His work by making a moment happen. The problem is, the moment passes, and if it wasn't an authentic work of the Spirit, there won't be any lasting fruit.

When a relationship with God has been built upon emotional experiences, students can talk themselves out of that relationship. The nostalgia of the moment ends up being replaced with cynicism, because, regardless of what they felt, it hasn't really made a difference in their lives, and this invalidates the experience. We all know the feeling of going somewhere we haven't been since we were very young. We have vivid memories of what the place was like, but when we see it again, the place is nothing like what we remembered. The park down the street from our childhood house that we remember as a source of endless fun is now seen as a beaten-up slide with a couple of swings.

There has to be more than big events, hyped-up experiences, and great moments. You can't sustain a moment, but you can sustain a conversation. We need to invite students into an important conversation about the Holy Spirit. He can be present in the powerful moments, but He also desires to be present in the ordinary moments of our lives. We need to help students better understand the person and the work of the Holy Spirit and how dependent we are upon Him for everything. So let's talk about what Spirit-dependency is.

chapter five

SHOW SOME SPIRIT

*C*razy games, high-energy church services, smelly cabins, below-average food resulting in above-average amounts of bathroom visits, new friends, more crazy games, and the dream of leaving with a girlfriend: summer church camp. I didn't grow up going to church camp every summer, but I went to enough of them that I began to notice a similar progression in topics for the evening services:

Night one: Salvation

Night two: Sanctification

Night three: Holy Spirit

Night four: Call to Ministry

It was as if the message was: (1) Get saved or "re-saved"; (2) now that you're saved, don't sin anymore; (3) now that you don't sin anymore, the Holy Spirit can come fill you, and P. S. things might get crazy tonight; and (4) now that you have the Holy Spirit, you can commit to being something amazing like a missionary in a dangerous country, or a youth pastor, if you're a wimpy Christian.

Obviously, I'm poking a little fun so let me clarify—God used some of these nights in my life in ways I still remember. God may have used a church camp in your life, and camp is an indirect cause for you even holding and reading this book. So I don't have an issue with any of those topics or the camp setting. But as we move into this chapter on Spirit-dependency as an indicator of health in your ministry, I want to point out two things that as a young, impressionable teenager became easy to believe because of how those services were themed and presented.

First, I thought that the Holy Spirit pretty much had only one role in my life: speaking in tongues. Second, by naming one of the nights "Holy Spirit night," the inference was that the Holy Spirit was missing in action the other nights. So I thought I needed Him for speaking in tongues, but that I could get through salvation, sanctification, and mission without Him. Nothing could be further from the truth.

So with those thoughts in mind (I think a lot of youth have the same thoughts), let me pose a few questions: Are we really helping students be Spirit-dependent when one night of our camp or retreat is exclusively "Holy Spirit night?" What are we saying about the other nights? What are we saying about the rest of their lives?

To address the tendency to evaluate the health of youth ministry by big events and emotion-filled experiences, let me suggest that we reconsider how we talk about the Holy Spirit and how we can help our students understand the life of the Christian in relationship to the Spirit. As you already know, the role of the Spirit in the life of the believer cannot be contained within one night, one event, one experience, or one church building— nor should it be!

Growing up, I would never have thought of the Holy Spirit speaking to me in my school halls, workplace, or bedroom. I was completely ready for the Spirit on Wednesday night of camp and at the end of Sunday night services (remember those?). Whenever something loud or weird began to happen in the service I knew who had finally showed up—the Holy Spirit. (By the way, why was the third person of the Godhead habitually late to church?)

In those intense moments, the Holy Spirit was for me like the crazy mascot at a sporting event. You know the type. Some sort of non-specific animal-looking creature that's running around the stands pulling pranks on spectators, rubbing his belly on the backs of their heads or taking their hats. It was always hilarious and enjoyable to watch as long as it was on the other side of the arena or at least in a different section from me. But as soon as Mr. Creepy Mascot came close to where I was sitting, I would tense up and brace for the worst—being embarrassed or made to

> *The role of the Spirit in the life of the believer cannot be contained within one night, one event, one experience, or one church building—nor should it be!*

look like a fool. I hate to admit it, but growing up I thought of the Holy Spirit that way in certain moments of church services and altar times. There must be a better way to help our students love, appreciate, and embrace the person and work of the Holy Spirit. How do we move them from emotional-experience chasers to Spirit-dependent?

For the next portion of this chapter, I want to take a closer look at the role of the Holy Spirit in salvation, sanctification, and mission (using the summer camp schedule as an outline). I want to consider how, by stressing the Holy Spirit's role in all three areas, we begin to cultivate Spirit-dependency. I doubt you or any other youth leader would disagree that the Spirit of God is intimately involved in all three, but I'm not sure our students get it. I don't know that your average youth group teenager understands the role of the Spirit in bringing her to saving faith in Jesus, or the need for the Spirit in the maturing of her faith. But before I get to that, let me make a few comments about the baptism in the Holy Spirit.

WHAT THE BAPTISM OF
THE HOLY SPIRIT IS AND IS NOT

In another book I wrote, *The Word and the Spirit,*[1] I addressed some misconceptions around the baptism in the Holy Spirit. I'm not revisiting that full conversation here, but it's certainly one worth having. I realize that not everyone reading this book believes the same way regarding speaking in tongues. Some believe that it was only for the early church. Others believe it's still for today, but not for every believer. And still others believe that speaking in tongues should be the norm for today's believer. For those who believe the latter, the lists I provide in *The Word and the Spirit* will help guard you from miscommunicating the purpose of the baptism of the Spirit.[2] For those who fall into one of the first two groups, maybe these lists will at least help you better understand the position—or at least what it isn't. Either way the teaching (or lack of teaching) on the baptism of the Holy Spirit can be healthy or unhealthy. I would recommend you check out chapter 8 from *The Word and the Spirit* if you're committed to helping teenagers understand the baptism in the Holy Spirit. Or better yet, read *Life In the Spirit* by Dr. George Wood.[3] If we as youth leaders are going to create a culture of Spirit-dependency in our ministries, we need a broad and rich vocabulary regarding the person and work of the Spirit—including the baptism in the Holy Spirit.

THE ROLE OF THE SPIRIT IN OUR PATH TO JESUS

Let's look at the role of the Holy Spirit in salvation, sanctification, and mission. As you read through this next section, consider whether or not your leaders and students understand these truths. It may be valuable for you to take some of the content below and teach through it to elevate the level of Spirit-dependency in your group.

Salvation

Most teenagers think of salvation as something that God the Father and God the Son cooked up. A vital part of Spirit-dependency is realizing that the Holy Spirit is involved in salvation. Below, I've drawn from *The Word and the Spirit*[4] to help explain the role of the Spirit in true conversion.

The Holy Spirit helps us know. And He helps us know the two most important things that anyone, anywhere, needs to know:

1. I'm a great sinner.

2. Jesus is a great Savior.

In John's gospel, Jesus said that the Holy Spirit convicts us of our sin (John 16:8–11). Not only does He convict us of our sin, but He also seeks us out in our sin. The first step to being a Christian is giving up on the idea of fixing yourself and realizing that nothing in this world, including yourself, can fix the brokenness in you! Unless the Holy Spirit intervenes, we'll never know that on our own. Because of sin, we're prone to use anything, and everything, as a source of false hope.

The Spirit pursues us when we are lost. He shines the light of the gospel into the darkness of our hearts so that we can accurately see our sin. He doesn't convict us just so we feel hopeless, guilty, and shamed. He convicts us because He loves us so much that He is completely committed to helping us know our need for a Savior. We tend to think we just need a little help along our way, when what we really need is a brand new start.

The Spirit is a key player in the work of salvation. I used to think that salvation was mostly about what Jesus did. I've learned more recently that God the Father, God the Son, and God the Holy Spirit all are integrally involved in salvation. Here's a brief summary that can help students understand how they work together:

God the Father saw humankind in ruin and, by sending His Son, He provided a plan to rescue the sin-filled hearts of humankind. Jesus was obedient to the Father and came to earth as a human to take our place in life and in death. He lived perfect as our substitute, and He died shamefully as the substitute sacrifice! On the cross, Jesus became sin so that we could become the righteousness of God in Jesus (2 Cor. 5:21). Then He rose from the dead, giving us the hope of resurrection. He took the full force of death so that we could taunt death with, "O Death, where is your sting?" (1 Cor. 15:55). The Spirit enabled Jesus to live the life He lived. He empowered Jesus to do miracles and healings, and signs and wonders.

> *The grace of God and the work of the Spirit awaken our hearts to respond in true repentance and true faith; it is the Holy Spirit who makes our dead hearts alive—through regeneration.*

All of those point to the kingdom of God coming to earth and the gradual reversal and eventual elimination of sadness, sickness, and pain for humankind and all of creation. This same Spirit raised Christ from the dead!

The same Spirit now pursues us, shows us we need a Savior, and reveals Jesus to our hearts! The grace of God and the work of the Spirit awaken our hearts to respond in true repentance and true faith; it is the Holy Spirit who makes our dead hearts alive— through regeneration. In the book I mentioned earlier, *Living in the Spirit,* author Dr. George Wood, general superintendent of the Assemblies of God, helps us understand the truth of regeneration: "As the Spirit brooded over the material creation of the earth and brought everything into being through His creative act, He is also at work in the spiritual re-creation of our inner lives."[5] We ought to thank the Holy Spirit for our salvation, just as much as we thank the Son and the Father for our salvation.

Sanctification

The church in Galatia had forgotten the role of the Holy Spirit in spiritual growth. They began to focus on their works and the human-centered ways they could establish themselves as holy. In his letter to the Galatians, Paul had some strong words for them: "How foolish can you be? After starting your new lives in the Spirit, are you now trying to become perfect by your own human effort?" (Gal. 3:3). The Spirit helps us grow by causing us to look back, look in, and look forward.

The Look Back

The first advocate is Jesus, and He speaks to the Father on our behalf. The Spirit is the second advocate ("another advocate," according to Jesus' words in John 14:16), and He speaks to us on our behalf. He is always whispering (and at times, shouting) to our hearts, reminding us that in Christ we are too "right" and too "rich" to be pursuing rightness and riches elsewhere, because those futile pursuits lead us into sin. The Spirit helps us grow in right living by reminding us of the truth and the cost of our right standing.

The Spirit also testifies about Jesus, which means He is always talking to our hearts about who Jesus is and what Jesus did. And He assures our hearts that it is all truth! The Spirit is like an expert witness on the stand at a trial, validating another person. The primary work of the Holy Spirit is to reveal Jesus to our hearts! Jesus told His disciples: "But I will send you the Advocate—the Spirit of truth. He will come to you from the Father and will testify all about me" (John 15:26). Check out Jesus' words in John 16:8–15 as He shares about the coming of the Holy Spirit:

> *The primary work of the Holy Spirit is to reveal Jesus to our hearts!*

When he comes, he will convict the world of its sin, and of God's righteousness, and of the judgment. The world's sin is that it refuses to believe in me. Righteousness is available because I go to the Father, and you will see me no more. Judgment will come because the prince of this world now stands condemned. I have much more to say to you, more than you can now bear. But when he, the Spirit of truth, comes, he will guide you into all truth. He will not speak on his own; he will speak only what he hears, and he will tell you what is yet to come. He will bring glory to me by taking from what is mine and making it known to you.

The Look In

The Spirit helps us grow by helping us look into our own hearts. The Bible teaches us that our hearts are wicked in ways we can't even recognize, and that we can deceive ourselves. We desperately need the Holy Spirit to examine our hearts and to guide us into truth. We also need Him to convict us when we sin and should be so thankful that He doesn't stop doing that!

Verse 12 implies that the Spirit not only reminds our hearts of the things that Jesus already said, but also the things that Jesus wanted to say. As leaders, we have to help teens understand that the Holy Spirit personally speaks into their lives, in a way that helps them grow into the image of Jesus. Unless the Spirit helps them look in, they can't grow spiritually.

The Look Forward

Consider what the apostle Paul wrote to the church at Ephesus about the Holy Spirit being a guarantee of what is to come:

> *And now you Gentiles have also heard the truth, the Good News that God saves you. And when you believed in Christ, he identified you as his own by giving you the Holy Spirit, whom he promised long ago. The Spirit is God's guarantee that he will give us the inheritance he promised and that he has purchased us to be his own people. He did this so we would praise and glorify him. (Eph. 1:13–14)*

Here, Paul teaches us that the Holy Spirit marks believers as those who belong to God. The Holy Spirit is a seal, like a stamp, upon our lives and our hearts. He is given as a sign of ownership. Verse 14 reveals that He is also the pledge and first payment for our final inheritance in Christ. The Holy Spirit is a pledge, or proof, that God will keep us and bring us to Him someday. The Spirit has been given to help us confidently look forward to that future day. Second Corinthians 1:21–22 says it this way:

> It is God who enables us, along with you, to stand firm for Christ. He has commissioned us, and he has identified us as his own by placing the Holy Spirit in our hearts as the first installment that guarantees everything else he has promised us.

The Spirit helps us look forward to the great hope of heaven and to the restoration of all things. He reminds us of heaven and eternal life in the presence of God, giving us strength in hard times. This hope of seeing Jesus face-to-face can fill our hearts with peace in troubling moments. The Holy Spirit reminds our hearts that God is making all things new, and that one day He will wipe every tear from our eyes. We grow when we look forward and rest in our future hope.

Mission

In chapter 7, we'll talk about mission, so I won't say much here. Just know that the power of the Spirit has a specific purpose in the life of the believer, which is to empower that person to live on mission. This purpose is evident in the words of Jesus in Acts 1, in the narrative in Acts 2, and in the remainder of the New Testament.

God's people are a people of the Spirit, and it's not just so they can be odd or even holy. They can join the mission of God! The power apart from the purpose turns us into an eclectic social club and nothing more.

Our students need to learn to live in the Spirit in every single arena of life. Nothing of eternal value will happen in us or through us that isn't directly tied to the work of the Holy Spirit. In the next few pages, you'll find practical ideas and tools for moving from events and experiences to Spirit-dependency in your youth ministry.

next steps
FOSTERING SPIRIT-DEPENDENCY

To talk about the vital need to foster Spirit-dependency in our students and not offer practical ways to start to do that seems pretty irresponsible—and lame. So this next part should give you some ideas and tools, as well as a look at practical ways youth leaders today are helping to change the conversation from creating big events and experiences to developing spiritual dependency in their students.

1. Talk to the Holy Spirit in front of your students.

This isn't nearly as wacky as it may sound. All I'm suggesting is that we credit the Holy Spirit for what He has done and is doing—and that we do it out loud. When you open or close the service in prayer, thank the Holy Spirit for His work during that night. How powerful would it be if every week your students heard you or another leader praying something like the following prayers?

- Holy Spirit, thank you for being a good friend.

- Holy Spirit, thank you for pointing our hearts to Jesus.

- Holy Spirit, thank you for sealing us for the day of redemption.

- Holy Spirit, thank you for helping us in our weakness.

- Holy Spirit, thank you for teaching us God's truth.

- Holy Spirit, thank you for not leaving us alone in our sin.

- Holy Spirit, thank you for pursuing us in the dark moments of our lives.

- Holy Spirit, thank you for producing real change in our lives.

- Holy Spirit, thank you for praying through us when we have no words.

- Holy Spirit, thank you for forming the living Christ within us.

Doesn't reading that list cause you to be more thankful for the Holy Spirit? I believe our students would begin to grow in dependency on the Holy Spirit if they heard us talking to Him more often.

2. Focus on conversations, not moments.

You can't sustain a moment, but you can sustain a conversation. I often remind youth pastors that the real value of the big event is that those environments have a way of starting, surfacing, or accelerating important conversations between students and leaders. At the end of a powerful service, be sure to take the time to connect leaders with students for the purpose of conversations.

It might be wise to think about making the next youth service a time just for conversations. Set up the night in a way that every student has the opportunity to sit with a leader or a group of students and share about what the days since the event have been like and what the next step is for him or her. This might involve providing your leaders and students with a few follow-up small group questions. Another idea is using social media (a Facebook poll question in a private youth group page or a Twitter or Instagram hashtag to categorize student's responses to a key application thought or question. Do anything you can to keep the conversation alive!

3. Explain and model biblical repentance.

Repentance is not simply saying you're sorry, feeling crummy about what you've done, or beating yourself up for your mistakes. True repentance is based on the realization that we've not simply broken God's rules—we've broken His heart. We have committed spiritual adultery and chosen another love over Him.

Repentance is not turning from bad behavior to good behavior. Repentance is when the Spirit enables us to see that the things we're treasuring and trusting in more than Jesus are causing our hearts to be grieved by our willingness to chase empty idols. But repentance is also the Spirit redirecting our hearts back to Jesus as the only One worthy of our worship. In repentance, we not only receive the forgiveness of Jesus, we also receive the assurance that we are covered by His righteousness.

For many students, "having a good cry" is synonymous with repentance. I've watched students appear to be sadder after they've repented—that's not biblical repentance. In David's great song of repentance, he prayed, "Restore to me the joy of your salvation" (Ps. 51:12), and "the bones which you have broken rejoice" (Ps. 51:8, ESV)! The final outcome of repentance should be overwhelming joy and thankfulness.

As leaders, we don't help our students when we try to model perfection. We help them when we own up and model repentance. If you lose your temper during a youth event, take that opportunity to humble yourself and repent in front of your students. And don't just repent of the symptom. Be transparent and repent of the sickness—whatever your heart was most desiring in that moment that caused you to kick a hole in the church van. Then express your gratitude to Jesus for His forgiveness and imparted righteousness. I guarantee your students won't forget that moment. (Your elder board still might want to talk about the damaged van, though.)

"I think it helps to be honest about my struggles. You celebrate that God is definitely using flawed people. There's spiritual dependency in our failure as well as success."

—**Rob,** youth pastor

4. Stop calling the singing time "worship."

Okay, so I might step on some toes with this one. But I have real concerns about the elevated focus on the singing portion of the service in youth ministry circles. I realize that singing is a biblical form of worship, and I'm guessing that no youth leader actually thinks we only worship through singing. I should also add that I'm a musician and songwriter—I love music, the gift of song, and singing songs about Jesus with other believers. But when we repeatedly refer to the singing time of the service as "worship," we run the risk of unintentionally communicating something harmful to our students. We end up reducing worship from a costly lifestyle to a high-energy sing along (Rom. 12:1, 1 Chron. 21:24).

At that point, teenagers get the idea they're worshippers of God if they sing their little hearts out for thirty minutes. They don't see and understand the truth that every choice they make is the result of being a worshipper. Youth ministries don't need to try to "create worshippers"—everyone is a worshipper! Youth ministries need to direct the hearts of non-stop worshippers toward the only One who is worthy.

Singing has become the primary metric for being a worshipper. We label people "great worshippers" if they sing loudly, raise their hands, or display a lot of passion during the singing time. It's a dangerous measuring tool and worth noting that people at most rock concerts look the same way. I'm not saying that passionate singing and expressiveness can't be a sign of a heart surrendered to Christ. They certainly can be. But we must help teenagers understand that singing is only one small way to worship. I would actually suggest that singing is the most self-gratifying form of worship a believer offers. Certainly much more satisfying than moments later when the offering bucket passes by!

My concern is that all the energy put into creating a great "worship experience" (especially the music) is actually creating a generation of young people who will gladly sing for an hour, but can't handle more than thirty minutes of preaching, three minutes of praying, and three seconds of silence.

To that end, I have two practical suggestions:

- *Stop saying, "Everyone stand up because we're going to worship" and start saying, "Everyone stand up because we're going to sing."* Don't misunderstand why I'm suggesting this. When we use the "worship" intro, it's incomplete—especially if we don't also use the same words to prepare students for the offering, or to hear the teaching, or to do their homework. I usually say something like, "Hey everyone, at this time we're going to use the gift of music and song to help focus our worshipping hearts toward Jesus." It might seem like overkill, but our language and narrative help shape our culture.

- *Consider breaking up your singing time to be both before and after the sermon.* I believe that singing is a very appropriate response to a sermon that points to Jesus. I also wonder if the mentality of singing four to five songs before our hearts are ready to hear from God's Word contributes to the idea that Christian spirituality is something we turn on and off. "On" when we walk in the church, and "off" when we're anywhere else—with the music helping get our switch into the "on" position. Worship as a response to the revelation of Jesus seems more appropriate than worship as a way to work myself into the state of readiness to hear a sermon. I'm not suggesting an either/or approach, but rather both/and.

By the way, one of the clues that music in the church and youth ministry world is becoming a bit of an idol is the fact that I felt the need to preface this point by mentioning I might be stepping on some toes. Another clue would be how many churches fight over the style of music. Let's not elevate music to the be-all and end-all of worship.

5. Create a "no expectations" zone.

Everywhere teenagers go, they face expectations of how they should act and what they should do. Teachers, parents, employers, and even friends have constant and unrelenting stated and unstated expectations. I suggest making your youth group setting a "no expectations zone." Let students know that there are many appropriate ways to respond during the singing and at the end of the sermon, but that no one is placing expectations on them to look or act like the person next to them. Placing and emphasizing clearly defined expectations on students might manufacture the "right-looking" response, but it also might have nothing to do with the work of the Spirit.

Being dependent on the Spirit means that we can trust the Holy Spirit to work inside students regardless of what it might look like on the outside. Let's not be so quick to tell or "coach" teens how to respond. Instead, let's create an environment where they can consider Christ and then trust that the Spirit can lead them to respond.

6. Celebrate the Spirit's work in the lives of students.

Instead of simply celebrating a student's decision or behavior, what if we took those opportunities to also celebrate what the Spirit is doing in them? It's good to tell a student that you've noticed how she's going out of her way to be kind to those who used to annoy her. It's even better to add to that comment something like, "It's so encouraging to see how the Holy Spirit is working to produce patience and kindness in your heart. I'm so grateful you're allowing God to develop that in you, and I hope you know that His Spirit always wants to do that in you and through you."

With the first approach, she feels affirmed for her behavior and credited for the change. In the second approach, she feels affirmed in her need for the Spirit and has the opportunity to watch you celebrate God's work, not hers.

"As a leader, I have to identify and reaffirm the ways the Holy Spirit is working individually in students' lives. One of the things I do with my young daughters is, instead of telling my six-year-old, 'You're a good girl,' I look for ways to reaffirm the Spirit's working in her life: 'I noticed you're working on . . . and the Holy Spirit is allowing you to be patient.'"

—**Mark,** youth pastor

"We want to celebrate the mission of Jesus, to tell the story of students who are being Spirit-dependent as a football player, a cashier. What we celebrate is what we perpetuate."

—**Rob**

7. Vary your response methods.

At the typical big youth ministry event, many sermons end predictably. A few minutes from the end of the talk, the musicians come back on stage and begin to provide some mood music. The lights come down. The speaker finishes with a killer story. Everyone bows their head, and they're given an opportunity to respond, usually by coming forward. This model has been meaningful in my own life, and it's one I still use.

However, I think varying the response methods helps students avoid becoming dependent upon a speaker's technique or over-reliant upon one response method. A new (even uncomfortable) response opportunity may help stir Spirit dependency in the life of the teenager. Here are just a few ideas to vary the response:

- Before asking for any response, sing a song that fits the theme of the sermon. In fact, ask students to remain seated while singing.

- Allow time for silent prayer while each person remains seated.

- Give students a specific prayer target and lead them through a guided prayer time.

- Give them a passage of Scripture to read and reflect upon.

- Read a passage of Scripture out loud, one line at a time, and have the students repeat each line out loud.

- Ask students to get into small groups to talk about what God's Spirit is saying to their hearts through the message.

- Give them a journaling opportunity.

- Take another offering for yourself. Okay, just kidding on that one.

The more predictable the response time is, the more likely students will fall into the rut of anticipating certain experiences. And one other thing I'll share about response methods: If you're Spirit-dependent, then the Holy Spirit gets to be the Holy Spirit and you don't. Our part is to make the gospel clear. Only the Holy Spirit can make the gospel real to someone.

Our part also is to ask students to consider the sin in their hearts. Only the Holy Spirit can convict and convince.

Sometimes I listen to preachers give altar calls, and it borders on manipulation. If you look to the quantity and the quality of the outward responses to validate your ministry or your preaching gift, you might tend to do or say anything to create a moment or a crowd. Let's be careful to not try to be the Holy Spirit.

"One thing I've been working through is giving students the opportunity to respond on a much more regular basis. Six years ago, I stopped doing [response times] altogether because I sensed emotional manipulation happening. I don't give an altar call every week, but I want to give kids an opportunity to assess their heart more regularly. Twice a month, I'll have an extended altar time or challenge the kids to look at their hearts."

—**Shawn,** youth pastor

8. Teach students that all of life is to be ministry.

I could write an entire book on this topic alone, but suffice it to say that I think we've done some damage to young people by calling certain vocations "ministry" and others "secular work." Scripture tells us all of life is ministry. Those who end up in full-time local church ministry are to equip the church for the work of the ministry, not do the entire ministry themselves. Regardless of your job or career, if you are a Christ-follower, you are called to the ministry of reconciliation.

The question isn't whether or not Christian teenagers are going into ministry, but instead where will they do their ministry. For some, it will be the local church or another country as a missionary. For others, it will be as a teacher, a doctor, a construction worker, an artist, or a stay-at-home mom. When we communicate that "ministry" is something you go to Bible school to prepare for, then we're also teaching students that pastors need the Holy Spirit to preach, but an architect doesn't really need the Spirit to design buildings.

We also create an unintended and unhelpful hierarchy of Christians: those who do God's work and those who are "stuck" doing secular work. The result becomes adults who don't understand the priesthood of all the believers, who grow bored with the "mundane" tasks of work, and who believe their only ministry is whatever they volunteer for at the church. Stay at home moms need to depend on the Holy Spirit as much as traveling evangelists. And everyone who has ever held an inconsolable baby while trying to make lunch for a toddler said, "Amen!"

9. Create bridges from big events and youth group nights to the everyday.

We all know that teenagers struggle after big events. They leave with the greatest of intentions, but they go home and can't follow up. They might do a few drastic things at first, but it becomes difficult to sustain. On more than one occasion, I remember friends going home after an especially convicting youth retreat and trashing all their secular music, promising to listen to nothing but Keith Green and Sandy Patti for the rest of their days. About a month later, they began the slow and painful process of buying them all back.

Here are a few practical things we can do to help create bridges from the big event to the everyday:

- Create or purchase a resource such as a guided devotional booklet or daily online video message. If you know the theme of the event in advance, connect that theme to the resource. Promote and even use the resource in youth group for a month or two after the event. This might help kids create a spiritual discipline that didn't exist before the event.

- Launch a small group cycle coming off of an event. Even have the first small group session at the event.

- Ask students to choose a leader to follow up with them for the next few months. Leaders can then find a weekly opportunity to have a brief conversation with that student, asking them what the next steps in their lives have looked like.

- Provide an opportunity at the next youth group service for students to share in front of the group about the personal impact of the event. Ask certain students to commit to pray for each student who shares.

- Have students write themselves a letter at the end of the event. Ask them to write about what they learned, what their next steps might look like, and what they hope God will do in and through them as a result of the event. Then have them place the letter in an envelope, seal it, and sign their name across the seal (so they know you won't open it, read it, and post it on Facebook). Have them self-address the envelope and then a few months later, mail the letters. I've done this, and it's pretty remarkable to see how God uses their letters to speak to them.

- If the service is about reaching the lost or sharing their faith, at the end of the service ask students to consider texting a friend who isn't serving God and simply say, "Hey, just wanted to let you know I'm praying for you." Most likely, that text message will create a future conversation.

"We want to give students a resource that parallels the event's message. If I'm preaching a sermon series, then we give them a devotional journal that relates to the topic so that they're engaging in community and then resourcing them."

—Rob

"We make a point of helping students get beyond themselves. We serve people who can't take care of themselves. Actually, taking care of someone requires you to rely on the Spirit. We put students in uncomfortable situations where they need God to succeed."

—Jim, youth pastor

"Whatever I'm preaching, I always conclude with questions like 'What does this look like tomorrow when you're depending on the Holy Spirit? or tonight, when you're by yourself? What does it look like to show God's grace to the girl tomorrow who will inevitably

hurt you? The idea is to take the focus off what's happening right now and focus them toward the future and how the Spirit works in their lives then."

—Mark

I'm sure you and your team can come up with other ideas to foster Spirit-dependency. The idea is, let's create bridges that help students move beyond the event to the everyday. Two keys to growth and fruitfulness are the right ingredients and the right environment. In disciple making, the two ingredients are the gospel and the Spirit. In the next section, we'll take a look at the right environment: biblical community.

Matching T-Shirts

chapter six.

GETTING ALONG ISN'T THE POINT

*T*here are some things you should know about *your* youth group."

I remember the moment when the dad of one of my teenagers mentioned that he wanted to talk sometime and then delivered that gem of a line before walking away. The word *your* is a funny thing. Usually it's entirely innocent, but in certain contexts it's incredibly accusatory. How many times have you walked in the door to hear your frustrated spouse say, "Wait till you hear what *your* little boy did at school today." In those situations, the word *your* serves as a bit of a spoiler alert—the subsequent anecdote isn't going to be a happy one. So when this dad said, "*your* youth group," I was pretty sure it wasn't going to be a conversation I would enjoy.

Turned out, this dad wanted to talk to me about the cliques in *my* youth group. His teenage son wasn't fitting in well, and the primary problem (he said) was the cliques and the secondary problem (implied, not stated) was my deeply flawed leadership. If you've been involved in youth ministry for longer than a few hours, you've probably had a parent, a teen, or a random person on the street bring up the topic of cliques. There was a time where it seemed like cliques were public enemy No. 1 in youth ministry. Youth workers had to spend half their time trying to break up the big, bad, scary cliques; even the slightest possibility of the existence of cliques was cause for Code Red, all hands on deck, crisis mode. Whenever someone asked a youth worker, "So what are you going to do about the cliques in *your* youth group?" the assumption beneath the question was clear: It's *your* job to make these teenagers like each other. It's a real pressure and one that we all try to deal with.

Think about the lengths to which youth leaders go to make sure everyone gets along—or at least looks like they get along. Maybe you'll recognize a few of these youth ministry usual suspects.

Team-building activities like ropes courses and trust falls. A ropes course is basically a series of physical activities involving . . . wait for it . . . ropes. And each activity is apparently intended to replicate situations you would never ever encounter in normal everyday life and put you in positions that guarantee you'll look ridiculous in any Instagram pics. But I would choose a ropes course over a trust fall any day. People with my physique (let's call it stocky) are not meant for trust falls. And I would never trust a group of today's Smartphone-owning teenagers during a trust fall. I can picture myself lying half-conscious on the ground looking up at two rows of teenagers scrolling through their Twitter feeds. I remember we always had a time during our weekly large group gathering strategically designated for the purpose of making the group interact with each other. It usually involved "Would You Rather?" questions, random pop culture trivia, or an ankle-breaking game like Train Wreck or Fruit Basket. If you grew up attending a youth group and you don't know either of those two games, then you should get a refund on your youth group experience.

Matching T-shirts. If you find yourself in an airport during the summer months, you'll almost certainly come across a group of teenagers wearing matching neon-colored T-shirts that proudly display which country they're headed to and what year it is. Before you see them, you'll probably hear them—it's as if none of them has ever been in public before. It's almost enough to make you want to pray for the country they're headed to. The Americans are coming; we're unreasonably loud, and our T-shirts are terrifyingly bright. But matching T-shirts has become a way of showing unity, especially in youth groups.

Drama police. You can always identify this youth worker because they're always having super-serious conversations with equally super-serious-looking teenagers in hushed tones before and after youth service. Being in the loop is their biggest concern, and as a result they're more up to date on the youth group drama than even the students are.

Spiritual attempts. The average youth group kid hears countless sermons on friendship and passionate talks about the need for unity. Growing up, our youth group would join other youth groups at area youth rallies where we were reminded about how we're all one family. But mostly we spent the time checking out the girls from the other churches and deciding how easily we could beat their group in a fistfight. It's not unusual for a youth service to end with students being asked to get in groups and pray together—the idea being that the group that prays together, stays together. As a teenager I remember singing songs about "breaking dividing walls" as the church held hands and swayed in unison (not actually as cultish as it sounds). I attended racial reconciliation services and found myself at events focused on the union of Jews and Gentiles as "one new man." I think most of the dudes were there to make sure that no one changed the official stance on the whole "exempt from circumcision" deal. Personally, I was more concerned about being exempt from the "no pork products" deal.

> I suggest that the more a youth leader focuses on simply making teenagers get along, the more the leader risks losing what is unique about true biblical community.

Once again, underlying many of these efforts was the thought that one of the youth leader's primary jobs was to make sure the teenagers all liked each other. You can probably guess by now that I disagree with that mindset. In fact, I suggest that the more a youth leader focuses on simply making teenagers get along, the more the leader risks losing what is unique about true biblical community.

In his book, *The Four Loves,* C. S. Lewis writes about the difference between lovers and friends. He uses the imagery of lovers standing face to face versus friends standing shoulder to shoulder.[1] We all know what it's like to be around a new couple—they can't take their eyes off each other. It's borderline nauseating. And nowadays—courtesy of social media—you don't even have to be with the couple to have your stomach turned by their incessant use of goofy nicknames for each other. Their growing appreciation and affection for each other literally keeps them close together. Yes, they may have shared interests, but that isn't the backbone of their relationship.

Friendship is different. It's built around a shared interest for something else—something outside of friends. Lewis explains it this way: Friendship is born at that moment when one man says to another: "What? You too? I thought that I was the only one."[2] This explains the immediate connection between strangers when they see each other wearing a shirt or cap supporting their shared favorite football team. They don't know a thing about the person, but they can immediately exchange a celebratory high-five. Admittedly, I may or may not have repeatedly hugged multiple random strangers in the bleachers of Yankee Stadium during game one of the 2004 ALCS playoff games (let's just ignore how that series tragically ended). Moms with young children have an immediate bond formed deep in the cauldrons of dirty diapers, near exhaustion, and endless episodes of *Mickey Mouse Clubhouse.* Youth workers can almost always have a conversation about their mutual frustration with demanding parents, challenges of difficult students, and an all-consuming disdain for lock-ins. Friends stand shoulder-to-shoulder gazing at the same thing.

So hold that thought, and let's consider input from someone else well-known by his initials. Author D. A. Carson writes in

Love In Hard Places that the church is "a band of natural enemies who love one another for Jesus' sake."[3] What an incredibly helpful thought. Next time you sit in a Sunday morning church service, look around the room and ask yourself, *Under what other set of circumstances would this particular group of people come together?* There probably isn't one. Teenagers visiting your youth group should be able to take one step inside your youth room, look around and think, *Why the heck are these teenagers all sharing this space and sharing their lives?* The prep, the jock, and the hipster can all stand together because despite their differences they have an all-consuming similarity. Jesus.

We all know that one of the reasons it's so difficult to love other people in the church is that Christians are far from perfect. (I would add that a number of churchgoers probably aren't truly following Jesus.) But another reason we struggle to get along is that the natural reason for getting along (the shared interests Lewis writes about) doesn't always exist—we don't have significant commonalities. We are different in many ways, but we learn to love each other for the sake of Jesus.

> *We are different in many ways, but we learn to love each other for the sake of Jesus.*

So when you consider and combine Lewis's thoughts and Carson's quote, I think you can see that outside of Jesus, Christians wouldn't necessarily be pals. Isn't it helpful to remind ourselves that our youth group is made up of natural enemies? Doesn't it help explain some of the ongoing tensions? And, more importantly, doesn't it help frame the solution to disunity? More on that later in chapter 7, but for now, consider the idea that what makes us part of God's family is not how enamored we are with each other, but rather how in love we are with Jesus! In Ephesians 4:13, Paul makes it clear that unity in the faith is inextricably connected to knowledge of the Son of God. And in Colossians 3:12–17, Paul teaches that Christ is the motivation for extending forgiveness to one another, the love that unifies us, and the source of our peace with one another.

We don't need to exhaust ourselves trying to get teenagers to like each other. What we really need to do is help teenagers better see and appreciate the Person and the work of Jesus. That alone leads to true biblical community. No community is more powerful than a community made up of Christian friendships built around a shared love for the Savior.

If we measure our group's spiritual health based on whether or not students appear to like each other, there are a handful of possible problems. Now please hear me. I'm not saying that it's a good thing if your teenagers fight all the time and can't stand each other. (If only! How much easier would it be to be a success in youth ministry?) I'm suggesting that the question "Do they like each other?" simply isn't broad enough, deep enough, or rich enough. Healthy relationships can be the outworking of biblical community, but a group of students who really get along doesn't necessarily guarantee biblical community.

Below are some of the potential problems that can result when we evaluate health based on this question:

1. It can stifle or stunt the growth of your group.

I never led a very large youth group. For us, gathering forty to fifty kids was a big deal. When we began to do that consistently, there was such an exciting vibe in the room. The students were excited to be there, and the energy was palpable—our youth group was the place to be. The group had such a sense of community— students liked each other, so there wasn't much drama (or I was oblivious to it), and even the leaders loved being together. But I noticed that there was very little desire in the group to grow. For the most part, they weren't inviting their friends to youth group; it really was the same group of teenagers every week. Eventually, something occurred to me: *Our students love the comfort and familiarity of this group. The last thing they want to do is invite people in and risk throwing off their group dynamic.*

As a ten-year-old, I remember the first time I saw one of my teachers in an environment other than the classroom. I was with my mom in the checkout line at a grocery store, and I looked over into the adjacent line and there was the math teacher I was not too fond of. Invariably, whenever I asked to use the bathroom, she made me use the word "may" instead of "can."

> *Me:* "Can I use the bathroom?"
> *Her:* "I don't know. *Can* you?"
> *Me:* "*May* I?"
> *Her:* "Yes, you may."
> *Me:* Takes the pass and walks to the bathroom dreaming of my retort, "FYI this is math class, not English. And if you really want to know if I *can*, I

would be glad to provide the evidence all over your precious desk!"

In the grocery store, in that moment, my worlds collided. I couldn't believe my teacher had a life outside of school, that she wore blue jeans, and that she ate human food! It really threw me off. Teenagers work very hard at keeping their worlds separate— it becomes a framework for identity development for them. They like to compartmentalize their church world from their school world, and the person they are at family gatherings from the person they are at their friend's house. So creating a world inside the youth group that is built around students liking each other (often built around sharing a narrow set of experiences) makes this world that much more difficult to surrender to the possibility of worlds colliding.

We exert a lot of energy into getting the group to like each other, and at times it might even work. But what happens when our group shifts from being "a band of natural enemies who love each other for Jesus' sake" to "a band of good buddies who simply like being together"? The lesson I learned the hard way was that the more my group grew to like each other for reasons other than a shared love for Jesus and His mission, the more likely they were to stop

The lesson I learned the hard way was that the more my group grew to like each other for reasons other than a shared love for Jesus and His mission, the more likely they were to stop caring about both Jesus and His mission!

caring about both Jesus and His mission! That's a big problem, and we'll look more closely at it in the next chapter.

2. We can cultivate fragile community.

This is one of the more subtle dangers when we zero in on the question "Do they like each other?" Relationships that should be shoulder-to-shoulder and focused on a greater shared love gradually become face-to-face relationships, focused solely on each other instead of on a shared purpose. The problem is that community built on likability ramps up the possibility of drama. When there's an unhealthy level of codependency in a friendship, any sort of hurt or betrayal that takes place between individuals has the potential to become *huge* drama. And the more inward-focused the group is, the greater the tendency for lines to be drawn, sides taken, and an entire group thrown into chaos.

If the community is built upon likeability, then one fracture will implode the entire thing. Understanding the true nature of biblical community helps leaders to both model and call students to rise above the drama that has the potential to derail a group. The best way is to keep the focus on Christ and His mission.

3. The value of the individual student is determined by that person's contribution to the community.

When what's happening in the room (the group dynamic) is more important than what's happening outside of the room (the mission), individuals are assigned worth based on their potential to make the group "better." That's when a hierarchy of youth group members emerges. Usually, at the top of the list are the musicians. The worship team members get the most attention from the leaders, plus the most stage time. They are contributing something significant to the cool factor of the youth service and, as a result, have high value. So when a talented musician visits the group, everyone works super hard to convince that person to stay and be a part of the band—they can contribute something great to the community. Conversely, for the kid who has nothing to offer (and even lowers the cool factor in the room), it's a much more difficult journey to break into the community. In the next chapter, I'll address how true biblical community reverses the values of our society, creating space for the outcast or the fringe student.

4. We can address symptoms instead of sickness.

When someone asks the "clique question," as youth leaders we tend to spring into action, identifying all the bad behavior in the room and requesting (or demanding) that it end—immediately! But if we simply address the lack of inclusion in the group or lack of kindness in the room, then we also might be simply addressing symptoms and not identifying the sickness.

Imagine you have a rash all over your body. You've tried ignoring it for a week, hoping it would just go away. But for the last couple of days the itchiness won't relent. The rash continues to spread, and young children are afraid to be in your presence—so you decide to see your doctor. You disrobe and put on one of their "gowns." I use quotation marks because there's no setting other than a hospital or doctor's office that you could get away calling those "wafer thin, basically backless, leave nothing to the imagination pieces of fabric" a gown. The doctor takes one look at you, leans back, and proclaims, "I know the problem here—you have a rash." You would probably say something like, "I already *know* I have a rash. Heck, everyone who gets within 300 yards of me knows I have a rash. What I need to know is what's causing it and how to treat it!"

Often the problem behind relational issues in youth groups is not simply that students don't like each other, or that those girls are mean, or those boys are rude. The real problem is they don't see and love Jesus as they should! The sickness beneath the symptom of exclusive cliques in the group could be the insatiable need to feel special and valued. In this case, students may try to create those feelings of value artificially by looking down on others and excluding them from their group of friends. Another underlying root in this scenario could be that they don't see themselves as having worth, and the best way to establish their personal worth is by belittling others. These are gospel issues.

Christ, the ultimate insider, was cast out so we could be brought in.

Only the gospel establishes our value and worth apart from the approval of others. We can't solve our relational issues by simply replacing the approval of one group of people with the approval of another. The only thing that breaks the cycle is the gospel's message: Christ, the ultimate insider, was cast out so we could be brought in. That beauty and truth has the power to free us from our frantic need to be an insider. In fact, if you're having community issues, you're probably having gospel fluency issues.

5. We create students who love the youth ministry but don't love the church.

I'm encouraged about so many things happening in youth ministry today, but one of the most inspiring things I'm seeing is this new generation of youth pastors' increased awareness of the dangers of creating a youth ministry silo separate from the rest of the church. When I first became a youth pastor, there was this unspoken mentality that "big church" was boring and lame, and youth group was totally awesome! The shortsightedness of that line of thinking became clear when we told high school graduates that they now had to go to "big church." Who wants to be part of something that has always been presented (directly or indirectly) as boring and lame? In hindsight, I realize that I was building a form of community that was actually counterproductive to the community of the church.

The danger of making the youth group setting all about getting along is that the group becomes reduced to a social club where I come to get my needs met and a place for me to share life with people just like me. Doesn't sound anything like D. A. Carson's definition, does it? In the next chapter, I'll further address the dangers of consumerism and examine the need for intergenerational relationships, but suffice it to say that teenagers who only love youth group and have no interest in the church are being set up for future failure.

I wish I could say that after the conversation with that concerned dad I didn't immediately go tell the teenagers in my youth group to stop being mean and to start letting his son hang out with them. But that's exactly what I did. And it worked because they respected my opinion, wanted to make me proud, and knew it was the right thing to do.

So does the end justify the means? I would say a resounding no. The most dangerous problem with my response to that situation and the "Do they like each other?" question is that outside of Christ, you can only appeal to self-serving or self-preserving motivations to convince teens to get along. You can leverage their ambition and their fears to manufacture a sense of unity, but that will do nothing to address the real sickness. In fact, it can actually serve as a breeding ground for more sickness.

We need to ask a better question then simply, "Do they like each other?"

Let's talk about what true biblical community can look like.

chapter seven

MISSION MATTERS MOST

*M*y friend Jōn is a youth worker at a church in upstate New York. He also serves our country as a captain with the U.S. Marines. Jōn served two tours of duty, one in Iraq and one in Afghanistan. The closest I've ever come to war is watching *Saving Private Ryan* in the comfort of my family room, but I'm curious about it. Combat is difficult for me to imagine. I'm always trying to get Jōn to share war stories with me. He has said he could tell me some of those stories . . . but then he'd have to kill me. And seeing that he's a battle-tested military officer, I don't take that as a figure of speech. But there is one interesting thing I've noted in the stories Jōn does share.

He told me that while he was in Afghanistan one of the things his platoon would do from time to time was set up and execute a meet-and-greet with a local city elder. The purpose of the meeting was usually to discuss something like digging water wells in the immediate area. So the platoon would go on a foot patrol to get to the meet-and-greet. The Taliban didn't want local civilians working with the U.S. military, so these meet-and-greets were always occasions for potential danger. Jōn explained that as they conducted their foot patrol, the team would be very focused and constantly aware of their surroundings, on the lookout for anything that seemed unusual. They moved as one and anticipated the unexpected—ready to react to any danger. There were no distractions. There was no confusion about priority. Everyone knew what needed to be done, and they did it. They were a team on a mission.

The people of God flounder when they lose sight of the mission of God.

Of course, the platoon wasn't always on foot patrol or involved in combat; there was down time. And Jōn said that when they were enjoying some well-deserved down time at the forward operating base, the soldiers' focus was quite different. During these relaxed moments, they tended to get more easily distracted. It wasn't unusual to find some of them setting up a tournament-of-champions type battle between spiders and scorpions indigenous to the country. Jōn laughs as he remembers one occasion when one of the Marines accepted a bet and gulped down some "dirty, sweaty sock water." Apart from a specific mission, their focus dropped considerably. It was inevitable and unavoidable.

As we journey into the conversation on biblical community, I think Jōn's stories are an appropriate starting point. The people of God flounder when they lose sight of the mission of God. Without a sense of urgency related to God's workings in and through our lives, internal conflict and general ineffectiveness are the inevitable fruit. Forgetting the mission can also create an inward-focused group of relationally-driven consumers. That is *not* true biblical community.

I've had the joy of leading about a dozen overseas short-term mission trips. I've led some great teams—honestly, I've never had a bad one. I would attribute that to the extensive pre-trip preparations, open and honest dialogue during the trip, and the fact that we developed a reputation for "accidentally" leaving annoying team members in terrifyingly sketchy places. Just kidding. I did actually leave two girls at a fast food restaurant spot once in Quito, Ecuador. We were rushing out the door for an impromptu ministry opportunity, and we didn't realize those two were in the bathroom. (For once, I was grateful that girls go to the bathroom in groups!) We were a couple of miles away before we realized they weren't with us. They were both fine and even still talk to me sometimes.

Because of the teams, the two trips that most stand out to me are Belfast, Northern Ireland, in 2006 and the Dominican Republic in 2002. The amazing thing about the team in Belfast was that it was the most hodgepodge team you could imagine. There were only fifteen of us, but we were from four different churches, and prior to the trip no one on the trip knew everyone in the group. It was an odd collection of personalities and talents, comprised of extremely quiet teens, adults, and college students with little athletic or musical abilities. In fact, the first time I saw them together I remember thinking *I've been pranked.* At any moment, I expected someone to jump out from behind a tree yelling, "Got you! Do you think we actually expected you to get anything done with this bizarre collection of random individuals?" Seriously though, I wasn't sure if this was going to work.

But something remarkable happened on that trip. To this day, I think it was the most effective and focused team I've ever led despite the fact that we had a pretty significant amount of downtime. In hindsight, I think I know what happened. Because the team members had very little in common with each other and because they didn't know each other very well (or at all) prior to the trip, there were no weird relational dynamics to navigate. Being liked by the others wasn't really on these team members' radar; it certainly wasn't a priority. These people had signed up to go on this trip not because of who else was going, but because they wanted to give ten days of their summer to serve a community that desperately needed the hope of Jesus. And this unusual team was amazing.

The Dominican Republic team was completely different. This group was all from the same youth group, and they knew each other extremely well. There was definitely potential for drama and interpersonal conflict. But I've never been on a trip where a team of students worked harder and complained less. We were up early, doing children's ministry all morning and into the afternoon, and then running church services every evening. And we did all this in the hottest conditions imaginable, nourished by gallons of water and very simple food (lots of goat and plantains) prepared by locals. We slept under mosquito nets in an abandoned-looking building, and our opportunity to take showers was completely dependent upon whether or not it had rained. Large buckets on the roof of the buildings caught the rainwater, and a garden hose served as our showerhead. When we did have a couple hours of downtime in the afternoons, we all basically passed out on the ground somewhere and slept—which was so wonderful except for the time my little brother passed out on top of a red ant hill, but that's another story.

Despite the preexisting conditions that could easily have led to a trip filled with personality conflicts and relational tensions, the urgency, work, and weight of the mission kept this team focused. I'm not saying the trip was perfect, or that no one at any time grew even remotely frustrated with someone else, but by and large the team was amazingly focused on the tasks before them. These students were so busy serving and sharing the love of God that they simply didn't have the time to get inward-focused or selfish. The pressing and tangible reality of mission trumped individualism and created an amazing sense of community within the team. Remembering these two teams makes me think of the words that Alton Garrison, assistant general superintendent of the Assemblies of God, writes in his book, *The 360 Disciple,* "Our visible love for each other and the world will identify us as the church of Jesus Christ. Our love for each other will allow us to overcome difference of opinion and controversial issues."[1] And the motivation for that "visible love" is found in a growing understanding of the love of God and the mission of God.

When I think about these two teams, I can identify two key indicators of healthy biblical community in youth ministry. One is that students aren't obsessed with their relational status

> *The only thing that keeps us from leveraging relationships for personal gain is an overwhelming sense of who Christ is and what He has done for us.*

with or within the group; the other is that the mission comes first. Now in the long run, the only thing that keeps us from leveraging relationships for personal gain is an overwhelming sense of who Christ is and what He has done for us. And in the life of any youth group, the mission that should come first is God's.

Let me be clear. This mission is not simply about getting teens to pray a prayer to have their ticket to heaven stamped. This is about God's mission to renew all of creation, rescue sinners, and restore God's rightful rule.

BIBLICAL COMMUNITY IN YOUTH MINISTRY

Drawing on my experience, as well as the good insights of youth pastors in my area, below are seven characteristics of what biblical community can look like in youth ministry.

1. Christ-centered.

True biblical community in any youth group must be first and foremost centered on the person and work of Jesus. Your teenagers should be bombarded by sermons, song, and conversations about who Jesus is and what He did. If a teenager can visit your youth group a few times and walk away with no grasp of what the youth ministry believes about Jesus, that's a problem. While it's easy to build a group on a central personality, there's real danger in building a youth ministry on the back of a charismatic youth pastor. First, you won't be there forever. What happens when you move on? Second, you're not perfect. What happens when the group becomes disappointed in you (and they will)? But most significantly, our admiration or love for our leaders doesn't make students right with God and help them grow in their faith. It's their love for Jesus.

Community is so much deeper and richer when it's centered on Christ, because we're constantly being reminded of what it cost Jesus to bring each of us into the family of God. In *The Hiding Place,* Corrie ten Boom shares her hauntingly dark story about how she and her family protected and provided for persecuted Jews in the Netherlands during the Nazi terror. A beautiful portion of the narrative comes when the hiding group of Jews votes to welcome a lady named Mary Itallie into their company, despite the loud wheeze from her asthmatic condition, which could easily have given away their location during one of the anxiously anticipated house searches. Eusie, one of the Jews in hiding, articulated the feelings of the group: "We're the orphan children—the ones nobody wanted."[2] Eusie knew they couldn't reject another because they themselves had been accepted despite being a danger to the ten Boom family. Perhaps Eusie spoke up because, as ten Boom noted, he was an especially unlikely recipient of welcome since his "features gave him away."[3] Christ at the center of any community means that we have a new way of sharing life.

2. On mission.

A common misconception is to think that "mission" is a once-a-year overseas trip or happens a couple times a year when the youth group serves at a homeless shelter or soup kitchen. I like what Irish author Christopher Wright says about our mission in his book, *The Mission of God,* "It is not so much the case that God has a mission for His church in the world, as that God has a church for His mission in the world. Mission was not made for the church; the church was made for mission—God's mission."[4]

The early church was marked as a people on mission—declaring and demonstrating the gospel anywhere they went. One of the key indicators of biblical community is that the group doesn't exist primarily or predominantly for the good of the insider. Many youth groups cater to the regular students—we want to keep them happy and engaged. But a group on mission is always thinking beyond the walls of the church. Maybe our focus should be less about ministry *to* teenagers and more about ministry *with* teenagers. In his book, *Exponential,* coauthor Dave Ferguson shares a quote that stuck with me from Austin Stone and Verge Network leader Michael Stewart: "We have realized that when you aim for Acts 2 community, you get neither community nor mission. But if you aim to pursue Jesus and His mission, you'll get both community and mission."[5] That certainly was my experience on my two most memorable mission trips.

3. Marked by a reversal of values.

One of my favorite Old Testament stories is found in 2 Samuel 9. David is king, and he is searching for any living descendants of the previous king, Saul, and his son, Jonathan. This sort of a search would normally be very bad news for the descendants. When a new king came to power, the last thing they wanted was a male descendant of a previous king hanging about. The fear was that the heir would eventually make a move for the throne. So they would banish or kill the descendants.

Well, news comes that one of Jonathan's sons is living, but he is lame in both his feet. His name is Mephibosheth (I know, poor guy). He comes before David terrified, probably thinking he's certain to be killed. But David remembers a promise he made to Jonathan, and he does three remarkable things for Mephibosheth. First, he calls him by name—establishing his identity and dignity. Second, he gives him land. Today's equivalent would be handing someone a huge pile of cash. Lastly, David tells him, "Furthermore, from now on you'll take all your meals at my table." This is really incredible—the king's table was no place for a crippled outcast grandson of an old enemy. It was reserved for royalty and for the cream of the crop. But David welcomed the broken. His generosity offers a beautiful illustration of what God has done for each of us.

Yes, David made a promise to Jonathan, and he honored it because Jonathan had been such a faithful friend. But God made a promise to us and honored it, even though we weren't faithful to Him. Why? Because Jesus was willing to be cast out so that we could be brought in. The gospel is the good news that God kept (and keeps!) His promises *to* us because Jesus kept our promises *for* us. And when we see the beauty and truth of the gospel, it creates a real reversal of values in our youth group culture. There's room at the table for everyone.

4. Intentionally intergenerational.

Biblical community isn't sliced up by demographics. I'm not interested in making an argument *against* youth ministry; however, I do want to argue for youth ministries that intentionally facilitate ongoing interactions between the generations. In 1 Kings 12, Rehoboam rejected the advice of his elders and instead went with the advice of his peers. While you can't use this text to teach that wisdom only comes from older people, you also can't help but notice that in this situation the older men gave the better advice.

> *When we see the beauty and truth of the gospel, it creates a real reversal of values in our youth group culture. There's room at the table for everyone.*

Creating meaningful opportunities for teenagers to share their lives and engage in conversations with senior adults can create real empathy for each other in the hearts of both groups. Finding ways for students to serve alongside adults might just heighten the likelihood that the young person transitions well into life in "big church." The handoffs between youth ministry and the rest of the church have proven to be a real concern. We've all heard the nightmare stories. Maybe the problem is that we wait until a crucial (and volatile) moment to try to build an intergenerational bridge.

5. *Willing to confront the rampant individualism in our society.*

A recent Pew Research project on global attitudes revealed results few should be surprised by: Americans value individualism to the point of believing in the power of the individual over the influence of outside forces. The study found that 57 percent of Americans disagree that "success in life is pretty much determined by forces outside our control." This is in contrast to 27 percent of the respondents in India and 31 percent in Germany; the global median is 38 percent. Pew Research reports that Americans value individualism highly; 73 percent of Americans say it is "very important" ("10" on a 0 to 10 scale) to work hard to get ahead in life. The global median is 50 percent and as low as 28 percent in Indonesia.[6]

The idea of the American dream has helped to create an inordinate hope in the individual; biblical community should challenge that stance. Our heightened value of individualism plus the vague notion of personal spirituality can lead to isolated "Christians." These people need God but not the people of God. In an October 24, 2014 blog post, "Why You May Be Tempted to Neglect Your Church," author and Christian ministry blogger Tim Challies wrote about the vital importance of Christian community: "Neglecting to meet with God's people is a sign of overwhelming and outrageous pride. You have somehow determined either that the gifts God has given others are of no real consequence to you, or you have determined that you are so gifted that you can happily survive without. The reality, of course, is that God has made Christians to thrive and survive only in community. Lone Christians are dead Christians."[7]

Confronting individualism also means confronting selfishness and myopic tendencies. In the parable of the Good Samaritan, Jesus invites us to consider a counterintuitive way to identify our neighbor. It's not about proximity—but rather opportunity. In Philippians 2:3, Paul instructs us to "be humble, thinking of others as better than yourselves." Acts 2 provides us with a glimpse of a community that went to radical means to care for one another. We're so individualistic to the core that we miss the opportunity to see the commands of Scripture as more than just a code of ethics for the individual; it's a new way of being a people. Author and missiologist Michael Goheen writes in *A Light to the Nations* that the Great Commission is "not a task assigned to isolated individuals; it is an identity given to a community."[8] We shouldn't simply call teenagers to go live on mission; we should form the very essence of our group around mission.

6. Affirming our role as image bearers.

Genesis 1:26 reveals that humans have been made in the image of God: "Let us make human beings in our image . . ." Notice the words "us" and "our." We've been created in the image of a God who has always existed in interpersonal relationships between the three persons of the Godhead. In other words, God has always existed in community with and within Himself. Since we've been created in that image, we're wired for community. Even before the fall, Adam felt an overwhelming need for relationship. Our desire for community is not a result of sin—it's how we've been created. Consider this: We'll still enjoy and desire each other's company in heaven.

Think how deeply wired we are to share life and experiences. Social media has made it painfully obvious. When I headed off to college in 1996, I ended up about thirty miles from another college where some of my closest friends were. Despite our desire to stay in touch and our proximity to each other, we barely saw each other, and we knew next to nothing about each other's everyday lives. I remember writing actual letters and mailing them—not email— mail! Like "handwriting on paper, licking an envelope, licking a stamp, and finding a post office mailbox"! But today I know what my friend in Europe had for lunch before I even get out of bed in the morning. I can flip through Instagram and see what outfits people are wearing today, how they prepared their eggs that morning, or something super interesting like a black-and-white close-up shot of the left side of their face. We can barely have an enjoyable experience without immediately wanting to figure out how to share it with everyone via social media. The reason we have these strong desires isn't because we're sinners—it's actually because we're image bearers. Now, obviously our depravity and sinful nature can easily corrupt this desire for community. You don't need me to convince you of that. How else do you explain all the pictures of cats on social media?

> *Confronting individualism also means confronting selfishness and myopic tendencies.*

Teaching on the Trinity and the nature of the Godhead gives you the opportunity to explain the source of our innate need for community and to affirm your students as image bearers. Let me add that it should lead to some important questions about what it means to be an image bearer.

7. Pointing us to the metanarrative of Scripture.

The big story of Scripture begins with creation and the fall. Immediately after the fall, we see the promises, the hints, the foreshadowing of re-creation. God is going to renew all of creation, restore His reign and rule on earth, and we get to be a part of it. God's plan is to form a people. In Genesis 12:2, God says to Abraham, "I will make you into a great nation. I will bless you and make you famous, and you will be a blessing to others." God chooses an individual through whom He will make a people, through which He will bless the world. It's through these people that the Savior ultimately comes to earth. God isn't simply saving individuals; He's forming a people to be a counterculture to the other peoples around them. There should be an attractiveness about the way they share life that causes others to want in. Biblical community is the way in which we get to live this out.

Teenagers want their story to matter. The surest way to help a teenager make sense of their story is to frame it in "The Story." Being a part of a youth group and a church isn't simply about having a reliable and safe social setting. It's about having the story of your life woven into the tapestry of the story of redemption. When we try to do the Christian walk outside of community, we might just be trying to rewrite God's story. The completion of this story requires the forming of a people.

So what does this look like in real life? The next few pages offer some practical ways to help your students move toward biblical community.

next steps
CREATING BIBLICAL COMMUNITY

I'll admit that I find biblical community more difficult than gospel fluency or Spirit-dependency when it comes to generating ideas for practical application. I'm not sure many youth groups are really wrestling with this one. I know I didn't. I tended to happily settle for "getting along." But what if we're called to something greater than singing "Kumbaya" and wearing matching T-shirts? And how do we get there? In this section, youth leaders and I suggest some practical ideas for creating biblical community. I hope these ideas stir discussion and thinking among you and your fellow leaders.

1. Evaluate the diversity of your leadership team.

We tend to think of relevance in terms of looking the part or knowing what's up, but relevance is mostly about authenticity. Knowing the latest gossip on Taylor Swift or being skilled in the art of using clever hashtags is not as important to teenagers as being real. Teenagers can quickly sniff out an adult attempting to fit in by wearing skinny jeans. (Actually, everyone can recognize those people by their unusual breathing patterns and the lack of blood flow to their feet.) We don't have to look or act like students to understand their world and to show them that we care. If your youth leadership team looks like they just walked off the walls of Hollister, you might want to consider the possibility that your students are missing the opportunity to get to know some amazing Christ-followers who don't fit a certain mold. Having youth leaders who are in different seasons of life and youth leaders with different interests and personality types gives your ministry a better chance of connecting with a wider variety of students. It might actually increase the likelihood that the leaders will help each other grow.

2. Create ministry opportunities for teenagers alongside adults.

This one is obvious, but instead of just forming student ministry teams, we should look for ways to strategically position students next to adults in ministry. Instead of having separate training days for the youth band and the church band, bring them together on one day. Let them learn from each other. The students may learn something about exercising restraint in musicianship, and the adults may learn a thing or two about being awesome. The same holds true for any ministry team.

I've noticed two things about the opportunities given to teenagers in settings like children's ministry. First, youth are often assigned menial tasks: "Oh you want to serve? How nice.

You can choose between being the person who cleans the glue off the top of the tables or the boogers off the bottom of the tables. Welcome to ministry." I would love to see teenagers get the chance to develop as teachers and to participate in significant ministry roles. Of course, this will require the adults in your church to be willing to intentionally and graciously make space for them. Second, the opportunity to work in children's ministry is often sold or promoted as the great escape from big church. Working in the nursery becomes the lesser of two evils; they'd rather do that than sit in big church for one more minute. This language just contributes to the mindset that youth group is cool and big church is lame.

3. Create mentoring relationships for teenagers outside of the church.

What about the students who have passions and talents that don't necessarily fit inside a traditional church ministry context? Maybe you could connect teenagers that are interested in science with a chemical engineer who attends the church? How about asking a Christian artist to spend an afternoon working with the young artists in your group on some of their projects? Or direct all the chubby kids in your group to the guy in your church who works as a personal trainer? (Just kidding! Don't do that!) You get the idea. When our students think that the only way we live life as a church together is by serving in traditional ministry settings, they miss the big picture. The body of Christ is called to share all of life, and all of life is ministry.

4. Offer ongoing local service projects.

While I still believe in the value of short-term mission trips, I increasingly advocate for youth groups to find local opportunities they can commit to for the long haul. It could be a soup kitchen, a tutoring center, a senior citizen home, or many other things. Find out what is already happening in your community and plug into it—you may not have to create something new. Serving within the rhythm of your local community is a great model for what mission can look like for any believer. Give your students the challenge of committing to a regularly scheduled ministry opportunity that stretches them and causes them to think of someone other than themselves.

"We emphasize the difference between hospitality and fellowship. Fellowship is something that happens between people who know each other. Hospitality is directed toward the outsider. We know our students are most on mission when they can sit down and talk to someone they don't know, who isn't like them."

–Jim, youth pastor

5. Do life together outside of church walls.

This one is obvious, but if your leaders only interact with your students during youth events and church services, then you're communicating to them that biblical community only happens when we schedule it or when you get inside certain locations. Use wisdom and clear instructions in how you empower your team to do this, but ask leaders to share life with students outside of church. This could be as simple as attending a sporting event or school concert. Encourage your leaders to visit your students at work—assuming it's appropriate. If it's a restaurant, coffee shop, or retail store, you can definitely visit them. If you have the opportunity to speak at another youth group or youth event, bring a couple of students with you. If you're a young mother and could use an extra set of hands on grocery shopping trips, ask a couple of girls from the group to go with you. Basically, don't do life alone.

6. Make your gatherings seeker-intelligible.

I wrote about this earlier, but it needs to be mentioned again. The clearest way to remind your youth group that the gathering is not all about them is to go out of your way to make it for the outsider. For example, explain the "why" behind everything that happens and preach like the room is full of biblically illiterate, unchurched teenagers. Be militant against "Christianese" and insider talk and ask everyone who takes the stage to introduce themselves. Celebrate the visitor and fight against any sense of entitlement for the long-timer. The more your group begins to function within a hierarchy of the haves and the have-nots, the quicker you'll drift from biblical community.

"Use ministry teams as an outlet for teaching, training, and mission. For example, we have a ministry team of guest services. We train them in the area of greeting kids when they come in, especially first- or second-time guests."

—Jeremiah

"I try to communicate the reason why they're coming to youth group and how that represents biblical community: You may be a junior or senior and have been coming for a while, so maybe your presence here is contributing to someone else's growth."

—**Mark,** youth pastor

7. Conclude your messages with a group-wide application.

In his excellent book, *Communicating for a Change,*[1] pastor and author Andy Stanley provides a model for the one-point sermon. In it, he suggests that you end each message with not only an application to the individual but also an appeal to the group. So if you're preaching on servanthood, then you land the end of the message by casting vision for what the youth group would look like if everyone embraced this idea of servanthood. It's an inspiring approach, and it prevents every talk from concluding with a challenge to the individual. When we always focus on the individual challenge, students lose sight of one of the key purposes of the proclamation of God's truth: to form a people. The truth of God's words carries amazing implications for the community, not just for the individual.

8. Find ways to serve the local schools together.

Every youth worker knows that the number-one "mission field" in the life of a teenager is the public school campus. One year, the youth pastors and students within the local youth worker network in Syracuse worked together to launch a dozen campus clubs in the fall. It was an exciting time that God used to remind us that you can't go wrong serving and loving your school. Students may not want to come to an after-school Bible study, but they'll appreciate acts of kindness. We worked with local bakeries to provide free breakfast in the teachers' lounges on National Teacher Appreciation Day. We adopted some of the less popular school sports teams and brought drinks and healthy snacks to players before their road trips. Our club learned about the other clubs that met at the same time and brought pizza and soda to them—all with the simple idea that the willingness to serve others in Jesus' name was something the Spirit could use to draw a heart. That simple idea brought our students together, not because they liked each other necessarily but because it centered them on the goal of serving their schools.

9. Preach on the relationship between the people of God and the mission of God.

I would guess that students don't hear often enough what it means to be the people of God and what it means to carry out the mission of God. Be intentional to include a sermon series every six months that addresses one or both of those topics. Believe that God will use your teaching to shape the minds and hearts of teenagers, transforming them from individuals into a people.

Jōn, my friend who served as a U.S. Marine captain, told me a memorable story. The platoon had a recreation room where they could relax and watch TV. The guys had a few favorite shows they enjoyed watching together. One day, just as one of those shows was about to begin, their commanders decided they needed to hook up a certain machine that helped them track enemy activity in the area of operations. This machine required an HDMI cable, and the cable they needed was connected to the TV in the rec room. You can guess what happened next. Well, the decision to take the cable didn't sit well with one of the marines, and he made quite a scene and wrecked the room. As a result, there had to be an investigation and a lot of time was wasted in the process.

It seems obvious to you and me that using the cable for military purposes was more important than using it for entertainment. But when an individual loses sight of the mission and cares more about his or her own agenda, everyone in the community suffers. The mission of God isn't an optional activity for the people of God. True biblical community is centered on Jesus and His mission.

"We have a buddy system for kids coming in, where we pair sixth graders with upper classmen, fifth graders with kindergarteners, etc. It gives students opportunities to mentor and be mentored—and become a community."

—**Shawn,** youth pastor

chapter eight.

PUTTING IT
ALL TOGETHER

A s I sit down to write the final chapter of this book, I can
look outside and see that fall is in full swing in upstate
New York. When I travel outside the state and people learn that
I'm from New York, they almost always immediately assume that
I live in the shadow of skyscrapers, ride the subway to work, and
will soon prove to be the rudest person they've ever met. There's
a lot more to New York than New York City. Where I live is mostly
a mix of suburbs and rural communities. So when I look outside
today, I can see the beautiful changing colors of the leaves and it
makes me glad. It's like a master painter has taken to the trees
and delivered an amazing result.

Fall is my favorite season by far. I was born in the fall, and
so was my wife—and we were married in the autumn. I love the

flavors: pumpkin-flavored desserts, warm apple dumplings, and cinnamon-scented hugs (I made up the last one). If you live in a part of the country or the world where you never get to experience fall, I'm sad for you. Fall is so fantastic it almost takes the sting out of our five-month winters and the fact that I spend a few days every winter shoveling my roof. My *roof!*

Fall is also home to my favorite holiday, Thanksgiving. A day of food, family, food, football, and food—what else could you want? And there's absolutely no hype around it, unlike the next major holiday on the calendar. We have a rule in my house about Christmas music—not a note of it until after Thanksgiving. Now before you label me a Scrooge, just consider that this still gives my family thirty-plus days to take turns listening to and singing songs either about fictional characters like Frosty and Rudolph, or songs loaded with confusing phrases about a real person (Jesus, in case you weren't sure). I feel like I've made my case for Thanksgiving. #RespectTheBird

But one of the main reasons I love fall is that I get to start wearing my fall clothes—my sweaters, my sweatshirts, and my hoodies. Fall is the time for comfortable clothes. Summer clothes (flimsy T-shirts and short shorts) are for the skinny people, but fall attire is for the rest of us. I like to call sweatshirts and hoodies the "great equalizers" of the fashion industry. If I'm standing next to a guy who spends more time at the gym than he sleeps and we're both wearing thin T-shirts, everyone knows I'm the slob. But if we're wearing our hoodies—it might take them a few seconds to notice the pumpkin pie stain on mine.

Good kids, big events, and matching T-shirts aren't the problem, but they aren't the solution either. And I'm writing this book to suggest that they might just be the "great equalizers" of youth ministry. From the outside looking in, people can't tell a healthy youth ministry from an unhealthy one so long as both have those three components. That might even be true for those of us with the insider view! So morality, experiences, and happy groups can mask deeper issues, prevent us from confronting hard truths, and keep the conversation on health and success far more narrow than it should be.

If you only focus on the question "Do they behave?" there's a chance your teenagers will turn into harsh legalists or defeated, guilt-consumed outsiders. If you only care about the question "Are they having the right experiences?" then you may create emotionally driven consumers. And if you center everything on the question "Do they like each other?" then don't be surprised to find a group of inward-focused social creatures. But if you build your youth ministry on the questions focused on gospel fluency, Spirit-dependency, and biblical community, I believe you will make disciples.

> *But if you build your youth ministry on the questions focused on gospel fluency, Spirit-dependency, and biblical community, I believe you will make disciples.*

I hope this book has been thought provoking for you. I'd guess that you've nodded your head in agreement at least a few times, and I bet many times you've stopped and thought, I'm not sure I agree with that. Thanks for reading on. I hope my heart, not just my thoughts, have come through on these pages. My intent is not to lecture (this is difficult since I'm a teacher by nature) or to discourage (this is difficult because I'm a New Yorker). My prayer is to enrich the conversations that you're already engaged in and to equip you for future conversations. I hope you didn't just skip to the practical ideas lists at the end of chapters 3, 5, and 7 (some of my youth ministry friends told me that's how they would read a book like this—some of my ex-friends, I should say). Hopefully, you have a few individuals or a team to help you process your takeaways.

CLOSING THOUGHTS

I want to end with four warnings, two verses, and one invitation for those of you wanting to move forward in gospel fluency, Spirit-dependency, and biblical community.

1. Don't look for a quick fix.

We live in a day where there's a simple, four-step process to being an expert on any given topic:

- Be a complete ignoramus.
- Google the topic.
- Read a Wikipedia entry on said topic.
- Expert status acquired!

You won't become an expert on these three values overnight, and there's no quick fix when it comes to changing the culture of a youth ministry. It requires the hard work of defining or redefining values, introducing and stewarding language, and shaping leaders. You can't afford to underestimate the work that goes into changing the conversation on health in your youth ministry setting. You can't rush it, and you can't fake it. You run a real risk to yourself and to those around you if you finish this chapter, close the book, and expect to be an expert.

In 2004, I helped lead a mission trip to Belfast, Northern Ireland. The community we served was quite impoverished. They had a large field for soccer, but no actual goal posts. Our team decided to purchase and install regulation soccer goals, and, on one of the last days of the trip, we played the first-ever soccer match there. I had spent the week kicking the soccer ball around with the local teenagers and by this point I began to have the delusion that I could actually play soccer. There were moments in the game where I felt like an actual soccer player. There was the time I kicked the ball and it actually sort of went where I aimed. There was the moment I was able to play defense without falling on my butt while blaming the below-standard field. There was even a time when I ran the entire length of the field and didn't require immediate medical attention. So I began believing a lie: I'm a soccer player.

I was standing with my back to the other team's goal when someone sent a high, looping pass to me. The ball hit the ground about three feet in front of me, bounced high into the air, and then ended up directly over my head. It was as if time stood still, and I had one of the most ridiculous thoughts of my life: I can do a bicycle kick! I mean, how hard could it be? All I needed to do was lean back, swing my leg toward the ball and let my natural athleticism and newly formed soccer superpowers take over. I envisioned the locals all surrounding me and cheering, chanting my name. This would be the moment that everyone would remember for years to come.

In case you're wondering what it looks like when a chubby American with no previous soccer experience and a two-inch vertical (how high I could jump) attempts one of the most difficult moves in soccer, I can assure you it's much worse than anything you could imagine. I almost knocked myself out! At no time in the very brief disaster did any part of the ball touch any part of my body. It was so bad that no one actually realized I was attempting a bicycle kick. They just figured I had decided to slam the back of my head into the ground as hard as I could or that I suffered from a violent form of narcolepsy. Once I explained to them what I was trying to do, they could barely contain their joy at my bravery. (I assume that's what all the laughing, high-fiving, and hugging was about.) I was right about one thing: That was the moment everyone would remember for years to come. The main mistake I made? I wasn't honest with myself about where I was in my soccer-playing journey. I actually thought I was a soccer player.

I realize that most youth workers will need some time to process and implement the ideas from this book, not because these thoughts are so deep or the product of special revelation—they're actually quite simple and central to Scripture. But changing the existing metrics in any long-standing organization requires a well-thought-out journey, not an informational memo. You'll need to create felt tension and a shared sense of urgency before anyone is willing to go on this journey with you. You'll need to wrestle with contextualization. You'll need to buy four more copies of this book to place in strategic places throughout your home (subliminal marketing alert!).

I hope by now that you realize this book isn't about giving you some ministry techniques to simply add to the existing model. When I travel and speak on these topics, I'm so encouraged by the resulting conversations with youth workers. Many of them have the self-awareness, transparency, and humility to admit that this will be a pretty significant paradigm shift for them. Go slow and steady, not fast and furious. And whatever you do, leave the bicycle kicks to the true professionals.

2. Honor the leaders in your life.

Paul warns us that knowledge "puffs [people] up" (1 Cor. 8:1, ESV). One of the great dangers of living in the information age is that we begin to discredit and disparage the generations that went before us. The emerging generation of youth pastors is better resourced; remarkably thoughtful when it comes to theology, ecclesiology, and missiology; and more strategic in their thinking than prior generations—including my own. I would also say they tend to be cynical and critical. They've seen the shortcomings of the previous approaches to ministry, and they're eager to be the first to point them out and, in some cases, fix them. They might even mean well, but it comes across as arrogant and dismissive of the reality that they're standing on the shoulders of the same men and women they want to cut down.

My friend and an international ministry leader, Heath Adamson, often talks about creating a "culture of honor." One danger facing young leaders is our tendency to neglect honor and default to flattery. When we leverage seemingly kind words and overstated compliments in an attempt to advance our agenda, flattery rears its ugly head. Flattery is self-serving in purpose and selective in distribution. But honor displays a humble attitude and employs gracious, genuine words (or strategic silence). The gift of honor is extended to leadership positions, not just persons in leadership.

As a leader, you'll always have other leaders to serve and follow. Often, leaders expect the people following them to trust them in ways they themselves aren't willing model with leaders they've been called to follow. At best, that's inconsistent. Whether or not you agree with our leaders, we're called to honor them—and not just to their face. It's easy to attack and critique leaders, but it's godly to do the opposite and protect and honor them. I've learned that my commitment to honor those over me is not truly put to the test until I disagree with them on a matter I care about strongly.

> It's easy to attack and critique leaders, but it's godly to do the opposite and protect and honor them.

I'm thankful for the ongoing work of the Holy Spirit as He guards our hearts and joins our conversations. I'm thankful that Jesus never failed as a leader and that His perfect leadership record belongs to, and speaks for, every believer! I'm thankful that the Father knows and judges the motivations of all men and women, so I don't have to. And I'm thankful for the grace to learn and internalize these truths.

The more you grow in gospel fluency, the more alert you will be to moralism. You'll begin to hear it everywhere. It's like when you're car shopping and suddenly it seems like every other car on the road is the same make and model as the one you're looking at. Nothing has actually changed; it's just that your awareness level is heightened based on where your mind is directed. But the irony about growing in gospel fluency is that your "handle on the gospel" can actually become an obstacle to you receiving the message of the gospel. Let me explain. Anything can become an idol, even your ability to understand and explain the difference between the gospel and moralism. If your growth in gospel fluency causes you to look down on and speak harshly of others, then there's a disconnect between your head and your heart. This doesn't mean we shouldn't look for opportunities to share helpful resources with others and prayerfully point them toward the authors, preachers, and ministries that have guided us. But it does mean that we need to ask God to help us honor the leaders in our lives despite our differences and to let the gospel make us humble and grateful, not harsh and judgmental.

3. Take care of your home first.

Every night at home, I say bedtime prayers with my daughters. One night I was praying with Lilia and in my prayer I said, "God, thank you for choosing Lilia. Help her to always choose You." After we said amen, Lilia looked at me and asked, "Why did God choose me? Because I'm good?" I wanted to take that opportunity to affirm what a good girl she is and build up her self-esteem. But I caught myself and used the moment to direct her heart to the gospel: "Not because *you* are good. Because *He* is good."

> *If you're married, then your primary spiritual responsibility is to your spouse and not to the teenagers in your group.*

My friend Tyler Sollie once encouraged me to think beyond three- to five-year ministry goals and to think about ten- to twenty-year family goals. Not just "What do I want my youth group to look like in three years?" but "What should I be doing today so that my children are serving Jesus twenty years from now?" Although many things are well out of my control (including the Spirit's work in the hearts of my kids), I still want to do everything I can to point them to Jesus, model the Father's heart to them, and help create a home where there's a marked dependence on the Spirit.

If you're married, then your primary spiritual responsibility is to your spouse and not to the teenagers in your group. Creating a disciple-making environment in your home should take priority over creating one in your youth ministry. There's no such thing as choosing family or ministry. Both are ministry, and your highest calling is in your home! I tell the youth pastors I work with, "Never apologize for choosing time with your family over a youth ministry event." When you're home, be present with your kids. Turn your phone off, set your computer down, and play with your kids. Ok, now I'm convicting myself, so I'll move on.

4. I take that back—take care of your heart first.

Everything you say and everything you do flows from your heart—guard it (Prov. 4:23). But we can't fix our own hearts because we don't even know our own hearts (Jer. 17:9). So what do we do? Thomas Chalmers wrote about "the expulsive power of a new affection."[2] His basic premise was that the only effective way to drive idols (lesser loves) out of our hearts is to introduce and receive a greater love.

As a child I remember the terror of playing the game Operation. The game required nerve, a steady hand, and the willingness to endure the inevitable indignity of that annoying buzzing sound. Every attempt to remove the Charley horse or the wishbone pieces was a heart-pounding, high-stakes adventure. Although I wouldn't suggest this approach because (a) it's against the rules and (b) it would ruin the game, imagine that a player puts the tweezers down and picks up a pitcher of water. As she fills the game board with the water, the pieces begin to float to the top and now are easy to remove. Game over.

Trying to break into our own hearts and remove all the broken, unhealthy parts is a bit like playing Operation blindfolded. I believe Chalmers is suggesting that the love of God is like the pitcher of water—it has the ability to so fill our hearts that it expels lesser loves. Practically lived out, this means being intentional to take time every day to meditate on the good news of the gospel through the songs we listen to, the Scripture we read, and other spiritual disciplines. None of these things can be done effectively apart from the work of the Spirit. We are truly and fully dependent upon the Holy Spirit to create a desire within us for the things of God. The other way we should rehearse and reflect on the truth of the gospel is

> Let the gospel, the Spirit, and the community of believers work together to guard your heart.

through the conversations we have, highlighting our ongoing need for biblical community. Let the gospel, the Spirit, and the community of believers work together to guard your heart.

TWO VERSES

One of the saddest verses in all of Scripture is found in the book of Judges, which I think is a pretty depressing book as a whole. The author writes, "After that whole generation had been gathered to their ancestors, another generation grew up who knew neither the LORD nor what he had done for Israel" (Judges 2:10). One of the central tasks of youth ministry is to make certain this same scenario doesn't happen on our watch. Let's continually remind teenagers of who God is and what He has done for His people. They might forget our sermons, our events, even our names, but let's do everything we can to prevent them from forgetting our great God and His gracious ways.

How do we do this most effectively?

Paul gives us a great model of youth ministry in his letter to the believers in Thessalonica. He writes, "We loved you so much, we were delighted to share with you not only the gospel of God but our lives as well" (1 Thess. 2:8). It seems pretty simple, doesn't it?

Step 1: Share the truth and the beauty of the gospel.
Step 2: Share your life that has been changed by the gospel.
Step 3: Repeat steps one and two.

AN OPEN INVITATION

I'd love to hear your discoveries, your struggles, and your wins— your journey. If we ever end up in the same place, consider this my sincere invitation to you. Introduce yourself, tell me your story, and let's celebrate the joy of being called out of darkness and into light, and being called to share that journey with teenagers. You'll probably find me hanging out at a youth ministry event, hunting down a great local restaurant, or standing on the sidelines of my daughter's soccer game. I'll be the one with the extra painful look on my face.

endnotes.

FOREWORD

1. Doug Fields, *Purpose-Driven Youth Ministry: 9 Essential
    Foundations for Healthy Growth* (Grand Rapids, MI: Zondervan/
    Youth Specialties, 1998).

CHAPTER 3: GOOD ADVICE VS. GOOD NEWS

1. Bryan Chapell, "What is the Gospel?" *The Gospel Coalition
    Booklets,* ed. D. A. Carson and Timothy Keller (Crossway Books,
    2011).

2. Tim Keller, *Romans 1–7 For You* (The Good Book Company, 2014),
    79.

3. "David Foster Wallace on Life and Work," *The Wall Street
    Journal,* September 19, 2008. Accessed November 18, 2014.
    http://online.wsj.com/articles/SB122178211966454607.

4. Paul David Tripp, *New Morning Mercies: A Daily Gospel
    Devotional* (Wheaton, IL: Crossway Books, 2014)

NEXT STEPS: CULTIVATING GOSPEL FLUENCY

1. Tim Chester, *You Can Change: God's Transforming Power for Our
    Sinful Behavior and Negative Emotions* (Wheaton, IL: Crossway
    Books, 2010).

2. Sally Lloyd Jones, *The Jesus Storybook Bible* (Wheaton, IL:
    Crossway Books, 2010).

3. Kerry Patterson, Joseph Grenny, Ron McMillan, and Al Switzler, *Crucial Conversations: Tools for Talking When Stakes Are High* (New York: McGraw-Hill, 2002).

4. Thomas Chalmers, "Sermon II: The Expulsive Power of a New Affection," in *Select Works of Thomas Chalmers, Vol. 4: Sermons* (New York: Robert Carter, 1848), 277.

5. Tim Keller and Edmund Clowney, "Preaching Christ in a Postmodern World" in *Special Seminars in Christ and Culture* (New York: Reformed Theological Seminary).

6. Stuart Townsend, "How Deep the Father's Love for Us," http://www.worshiptogether.com/songs/songdetail.aspx?iid=577430.

CHAPTER 5: SHOW SOME SPIRIT

1. David Hertweck, *The Word and the Spirit: Discovering How the Power of Scripture and the Holy Spirit Work in Your Life* (Springfield, MO: Gospel Publishing House, 2015).

2. Ibid., chapter 8.

3. George O. Wood, *Living in the Spirit: Drawing Us to God, Sending Us to the World* (Springfield, MO: Gospel Publishing House, 2009).

4. Hertweck, chapter 8.

5. Wood, 37.

CHAPTER 6: GETTING ALONG ISN'T THE POINT

1. C. S. Lewis, *The Four Loves* (Orlando, FL: Harcourt, Inc., 1960), 91.

2. Ibid., 96.

3. D. A. Carson, *Love in Hard Places* (Wheaton, IL: Crossway Books, 2002), 61.

CHAPTER 7: MISSION MATTERS MOST

1. Alton Garrison, *The 360 Disciple: Discipleship Going Full Circle* (Springfield, MO: Gospel Publishing House, 2009).

2. Corrie Ten Boom, with Elizabeth Sherrill and John Sherrill, *The Hiding Place* (Peabody, MA: Hendrickson Publishers, Inc., 2006), 120.

3. Ibid., 112.

4. Christopher J. H. Wright, *The Mission of God: Unlocking the Bible's Grand Narrative* (Downers Grove, IL: InterVarsity Press, 2006), 62.

5. Dave Ferguson and Jon Ferguson, *Exponential: How You and Your Friends Can Start a Missional Church Movement* (Grand Rapids, MI: Zondervan, 2010), 95.

6. "Emerging and Developing Economies Much More Optimistic than Rich Countries about the Future," *Pew Research Global Attitudes Project,* October 9, 2014, http://www.pewglobal. org/2014/10/09/emerging-and-developing-economies-much-more-optimistic-than-rich-countries-about-the-future/.

7. Tim Challies, "Why You May Be Tempted to Neglect Your Church," *Challies.com: Informing the Reforming* (blog), October 20, 2014, http://www.challies.com/christian-living/why-you-may-be-tempted-to-neglect-your-church.

8. Michael W. Goheen, *A Light to the Nations: The Missional Church and the Biblical Story* (Grand Rapids, MI: Baker Academic, 2011), 115.

NEXT STEPS: CREATING BIBLICAL COMMUNITY

1. Andy Stanley and Lane Jones, *Communicating for a Change: Seven Keys to Irresistible Communication* (Colorado Springs, CO: Multnomah Books, 2006).

2. Chalmers, 277.

ACKNOWLEDGEMENTS

1. G. K. Chesterton, *The Collected Works of G.K. Chesterton Vol. 20* (San Francisco: Ignatius Press, 2001).

acknowledgements.

G. K. Chesterton once wrote, "I would maintain that thanks are the highest form of thought."[1] If he's correct—and he just might be—that explains why this book was downhill all the way from chapter 1.

When you write your first book you can only hope to have an editor as gracious and gifted as Lindy Lowry. Lindy, thanks for dealing with this amateur and helping to shape this book. Thanks also to the entire team at My Healthy Church. It's an honor to partner with a team so passionately committed to resourcing leaders and churches.

When I was a teenager I had youth leaders in Lou and Barb Gonzalez who believed in me more than they probably should have. Lou was the first person to tell me that I would write a book someday. Lou, I guess you can officially tell me, "I told you so." Thank you.

So many other individuals in my home church have been hugely influential in my life and present in my successes and failures, loving me and pointing me to Jesus every step of the way. I wish I could list you all by name here—I hope you know who you are. I certainly do.

I have the great privilege of serving in New York alongside some amazing leaders. Duane, Bill, Bob, Larry, Dave, and many other remarkable leaders, thanks for allowing me to learn from you. I'm so grateful to the amazing youth workers in New York. Sharing life and ministry with each of you is a joy. A special thank-you to those who contributed their voice and input to this project.

Garland Owensby, thanks for walking through this journey with me. Your willingness to read these chapters was almost as valuable as your needed feedback—both encouraged me along the way.

Doug Fields, thanks for graciously lending your voice to this book. You are both a champion and model for youth workers, healthy marriages, and great families—I'm glad to call you friend.

Heath Adamson, thank you for "never forgetting what it's like to be lost." That's the starting point for gospel fluency—you model it so well. Scotty Gibbons, thanks for surprising me with your humility and graciousness. You have both encouraged me during this process with your leadership and friendship.

I'm a man blessed with the greatest of friends. Since I can't list all your names here, I'll just leave an empty spot where I can write your names in later. So thank you, _____. Between you and me, you're the smartest, funniest, best-looking friend I have.

Lisa and Josh, everyone should have a sister and brother as great as each of you. Thanks for being my friends. Thanks and lots of love also to my in-laws, aunts, uncles, cousins, and on and on. I have a beautiful family.

Mom and Dad, where do I start? You've always led lives marked by the truth of the gospel and the nearness of the Spirit. I cannot adequately express my thankfulness for your countless prayers, constant support, and unconditional love. Thank you, thank you, thank you.

Lilia, Caraline, and Madelaine, Mommy and Daddy love you girls so much. We thank God for giving you to us. Our prayer is that you will always love and follow Jesus.

Erin, you are the most generous mom, gracious wife, and gorgeous woman in the world. I thank God for you and for every moment I spend with you.

Father, thank you for the promise that you are making all things new.

Spirit, thank you for pointing my wandering heart to Jesus.

Jesus, thank you for rescuing sinners like this man.

about the author.

S ince February 2011, David Hertweck has served the New York Assemblies of God as the director of youth ministry. Previously, he served as a youth pastor for twelve years in upstate New York. David graduated from Elim Bible Institute where he majored in biblical studies with a focus in worship leadership. He is currently completing graduate work at Northeastern Seminary for his MA in transformational leadership.

David is passionate about helping local church youth workers create and sustain disciple-making environments marked by gospel fluency, Spirit-dependency and biblical community. He is married to Erin and they have three daughters: Lilia, Caraline, and Madelaine. David loves his girls, his family, good music, good food, his Weber grill, his Taylor guitar, Liverpool Football Club, the Yankees, and the gospel.

for more information

For more information on these and other
valuable resources visit www.myhealthychurch.com